Homecoming

Contextualizing, Materializing, and Practicing the Rural in China

Edited by
Joshua Bolchover, Christiane Lange,
and John Lin

DEPARTMENT OF ARCHITECTURE
THE UNIVERSITY OF HONG KONG

gestalten

Homecoming

Preface

*by Joshua Bolchover, Christiane Lange,
and John Lin*

The idea for Homecoming originated during the Chengdu Biennale in September 2011. The theme "Holistic Realm: Gardens/ Cities/ Architecture" called for strategies responding to Chengdu City's stated ambition to become a "modern world garden city." This call for harmony between man and his environment, architecture, and nature reflects a preoccupation long present in Chinese history. In response to this theme we presented a 12-meter-long cross-section from rural to urban territory, made up of multiple images from our project sites in China. This panoramic view illustrated many contested and indeterminate spaces that characterize the urbanization process. For us, taking a "holistic" view did not equate to a "harmonious" result—in fact, it was quite the opposite.

During the biennale, we discovered that there was a lot of common ground among the participants in their attitudes and agendas regarding their working experiences in China. We sensed an inherent tension between these architects to balance making contemporary architecture within a context of unrestrained development. There were different responses to this dilemma. Many of the architects looked to rural, traditional buildings or material techniques for inspiration. Some incorporated rural typologies into proposals for the city. Others began to build exclusively in rural areas, drawn by the social imperative of such an endeavor. By responding to specific issues of Chinese rural and urban development their work is contemporary and distinct; forming a basis for an alternative mode of architectural practice. This work and its underlying discourse, was the foundation for developing this project.

Homecoming is intentionally controversial and can be understood from multiple positions. It can refer to a generation of architects who are *coming home* after studying abroad, or are *going home* to rediscover rural traditions as a counterpoint to predominantly urban practices. *Homecoming* articulates a unique characteristic of Chinese culture which, despite its diasporic and migratory nature, is tied back to one's ancestral village. Additionally, the literal translation of *homecoming* is associated with a Maoist dictum during the Cultural Revolution to go "up to the mountains and down to the countryside." This piece of propaganda and related policy resulted in hundreds of thousands of urban youth being sent to work in rural villages. The same term is also inferred in the "return home" card, a special pass allowing Hong Kong citizens to travel freely into China. Symbolically this was instituted after the British handover in 1997 when Hong Kong was returned back to the motherland. *Homecoming* acts as a provocation and reminder that the rural in China is highly political, is contested, and can be seen from both a very pessimistic and idealistic point of view.

By asking "What are the specific Chinese conditions that matter most for your practice?" the foreword "Questions Please," by Yung Ho Chang emphasizes the need for a diversity of responses and inquiry to address contemporary Chinese architecture. Under the section Contextualizing the Rural, essays describe the historical evolution of the Chinese countryside, its shifting identity, and its interpretation through different modes of cultural production. Materializing the Rural portrays contemporary design philosophies which incorporate, extract, or adapt traditional material and construction methods. Practicing the Rural demonstrates alternative design methods to engage and activate rural communities and how the rural context itself can be a rich source for experimentation.

To explore the multiple positions of Homecoming in China the book is discursive, ending in a final debate of the many emergent issues that will affect the future of the Chinese countryside.

The architect as a critic, enabler or visionary is still a relatively new concept in post-Mao China. The advancement of this role and the impact this will have on contemporary Chinese architecture will result not from a shared cultural identity or formal similarity but through engagement with the prescient and urgent issues shaping China's urban-rural evolution.

The content presented in this book is the result of the Homecoming Symposium held at the University of Hong Kong in April 2012. It is thanks to the financial and logistical support of the Department and the Faculty of Architecture that this book is possible. We are especially grateful to the contributors for their open and sincere participation and their willingness to share personal views and experiences of the Chinese countryside.

Content

B—Materializing the Rural

Gallery

C—Practicing the Rural

D—Debate

Appendix

Questions Please

Foreword

Yung Ho Chang

What is contemporary Chinese architecture? This is a question that may not have an answer, or at least, not an answer that the majority of architects working in China can agree on. However, this doesn't mean it is a question one shouldn't ask, as my friend Ackbar Abbas, a comparative literature scholar, once suggested to me. A number of architects, both local and global, are asking that very question, each in their own unique way. Trying to define the nature of contemporary Chinese architecture was exactly why the participating group of architects, theorists and historians gathered together at the Homecoming Symposium at the University of Hong Kong in April 2012. I myself was one of the contributors on that occasion. Through exchanging our designs, more so than our words, I believe we debated the question that opened this paragraph without it actually being explicitly raised.

Curiously, although the symposium was a discussion about architecture in a particular region, the word regionalism, "critical" or not, was hardly uttered. Perhaps there was even a conscious effort to avoid using such terminology? Even so, and for sure I was one, there is no doubt that the Homecoming architects were influenced by the notion of Critical Regionalism.[1]

One reason why we no longer see what we do as manifestations of Critical Regionalism may have to do with the fact that today the formal language of Western Modernism is widely accepted in China. To this extent, the line between local and global is blurred. To achieve a genuinely local response, one has to go beyond form and investigate the contextual conditions at a much deeper level, including: availability of materials and technology, skills of construction, changes in lifestyle, grassroots activism, government agendas, the economy, and speed. These go hand in hand with issues of architectural tradition and culture. This means we are ultimately faced with different challenges today than the Critical Regionalists were in the past.

Another possible reason might be the lack of interest in any collective regional identity on the part of the architects. Individuality is presently a much bigger concern, given the not unusual experience of studying abroad and the wide dissemination of international media that has produced similar stylistic sensibilities among Chinese architects.

The contemporary state of Chinese architecture has no definitions but many voices and many questions. It is of paramount importance that we explore designs that provoke questions concerning the state of architecture in China, and make sincere Sisyphean attempts to answer them, in order to create a common ground for meaningful and constructive discussion and debate. However difficult it may be, discourse is more productive than consent.

I have no idea how many questions the Homecomers mutually shared at the symposium but in retrospect one can certainly detect them while reading this volume. The Homecoming symposium and this book may well serve as an introductory effort towards pooling these questions, debating them, and developing more.

May I ask: What are the specific Chinese conditions that matter most for your practice?

---

(1)   Kenneth Frampton, "Towards a Critical Regionalism: Six Points for an Architecture of Resistance," in: *The Anti-Aesthetic. Essays on Postmodern Culture*, edited by Hal Foster, Bay Press, Seattle 1983.

"What Chinese conditions matter most for your practice?"

A

Contextualizing the Rural

Despite dramatic cultural, economic, and political shifts over the course of the twentieth century, perceptions of the Chinese countryside as a pure and uncontaminated locus of Chinese national identity have endured. As a source of architectural debate and inspiration, the rural remains a relatively unexplored topic. How have concepts of the Chinese rural influenced Chinese architectural practice over time? To what extent does the rural remain a viable and effective discursive, formal and spatial foil to China's urban development today?

Back to the Village

Position by Cole Roskam

"Goodness develops only in the village, evil in the city. The city is the place of commerce and trade. People relate to one another with the aim of making profit. They are superficial and pretentious. As a result the city is a sink of inequities. The village is different." [1] Gu Yanwu, seventeenth-century scholar-official

The Chinese countryside has long signified more than physical landscape. It has also represented deeply contested ideological terrain. This is particularly evident in a brief look at the ways in which urban and rural China have been categorized, defined, and delineated over much of the twentieth century. From the fall of the Qing dynasty to the establishment of the Republic of China, and subsequently followed by the founding of the People's Republic of China, rhetorical distinctions between the city and the countryside have been employed by officials, ideologues, and intellectuals alike in an effort to locate the site and source of a uniquely Chinese national identity.

Architecture has played an active role in these efforts. More than other forms of cultural production, it is buildings that have helped to formalize the imagined lines drawn between China's cities and its countryside by giving each a visible material, tectonic, and spatial distinctiveness. Following the demise of the Qing government in 1911, for example, Chinese intellectuals inspired by an urban-inspired "New Culture" cosmopolitanism dismissed the dilapidated condition of Chinese vernacular construction as a means of distancing themselves and their movement from imperial rule. Over the course of the 1930s, however, perspectives shifted. With approximately 300 million of China's estimated 450 million people living in the country's rural areas, no viable reform movement could succeed without embracing the countryside in substantial and productive ways. Nationalists and Communists alike subsequently embraced the countryside in an effort to position themselves as the heirs to the true wellspring of China's cultural essence, giving rise to an era of Chinese "rural modernity."[2]

It is within this era that Zhu Tao's recontextualization of Liang Sicheng's expeditions through the Hebei and Shanxi countryside in search of long-forgotten Tang- and Song-era architectural monuments need be considered. His Odysseus-like treks through rural China have been extolled, not only as a search for remnants of some unadulterated Chinese architectural heritage, but for some authentic origin-point in China's architectural identity, creating a powerful mythology that continues to impact our understanding of Liang and the country's architectural history today.

After 1949, linkages between the Chinese countryside, the perceived purity of vernacular construction, and nationalistic notions of genuine *Chineseness* endured. Mao exhorted rural residents to ensure that their villages continue to surround the cities in a tactical effort to isolate and contain undue imperial residue, regardless of how industrially valuable China's urban areas continued to be, vis-à-vis the country's overall economy. Widely published plans of the Chairman's own childhood home, in Shaoshan, at the time may have burnished the Chairman's own celebrated rural origins, but as Frank Dikötter reminds us, romanticized visions of bustling, rural courtyard homes belied failures in leadership so catastrophic they led to people literally eating their own dwellings to survive.[3]

Mao's death in 1976 and the reascension of Deng Xiaoping in 1978 may have prompted extraordinary economic reform, but they did not sever the Party's deep ideological roots in rural China's "native soil" as opposed to its soiled urban environments. Drawing familiar distinctions between the city and the countryside helped to distract the populace from the radicalism of Deng's own policies, as suggested by persistent Party campaigns denouncing the bourgeois liberalization and Western-influenced spiritual pollution of the city in 1981, 1983, 1987, and again in 1989, despite the significant political and economic benefits wrought by urbanization. Here, too, the built environment unwittingly aided in these efforts; Robin Visser notes in her own recollections of post-reform China that distinct architectural change did not visibly manifest itself in the countryside until the early 1990s, a delay that obscured the official shift towards privatization begun years earlier.

In reality, Chinese cities have never been completely separate from the rural areas that support and surround them, nor has the countryside truly prospered without urban patronage. Yet as history suggests, every revolution needs a foil to justify its own creation. Philip Tinari's essay suggests that the idiomatic reemployment of the rural in several noteworthy examples of contemporary Chinese artistic educational and professional practice has the potential, for better or worse, to transform not only where but how an entire cultural industry works. For the architects highlighted in this volume, too, the countryside offers novel conditions and a useful construct through which some literal and conceptual distance from the creep of China's cities has been gained. In many ways, the most dynamic architectural work being produced in China today engages with rural as well as urban landscape in ways that eschew the normative, see-sawing dialectic between the two in search of some fragile but intractable symbiosis. Architects who willfully sentimentalize the rural deny what is a vital tangle of social and economic bonds that connect city, country, and the vast stretches of space in-between. Such nostalgia also ignores the entrenched politics at work in how contestation between city and countryside first arose in China, why it perseveres, and architecture's supporting and symbolic role in that history. You can never go home again.

(1) Quoted in David Zweig, *Agrarian Radicalism in China, 1968–1981*, Cambridge (US) 1989, pg. 19.
(2) See, for example, Margherita Zanasi, "Far from the Treaty Ports: Fang Xianting and the Idea of Rural Modernity in 1930s China." *Modern China* 30, no. 1 January 2004, pp. 113–146.
(3) See Liu Dunzhen, *Zhongguo zhu zhai gai shuo*, Beijing 1957, pg. 91.

◀ Liang, Lin, and
their colleagues
looking for
Foguang Temple,
a Tang structure
in the Wutai
Mountains, 1937.

To Search High and Low

Liang Sicheng, Lin Huiyin, and China's Architectural Historiography 1932–1946

by Zhu Tao

1932—A Year of Significance

In the West, 1932 was the year that modernist architecture, labeled the "International Style" by Hitchcock and Johnson in their exhibition at the Museum of Modern Art, gained new momentum, spreading its influence throughout the world. Partially in reaction to the swift development of modernism in China, 1932 also became a defining moment for the historiography of Chinese architecture. Liang Sicheng and Lin Huiyin, two young architectural historians, published separate essays in the March issue of the *Bulletin of the Society for Research in Chinese Architecture*, establishing an intellectual blueprint that would guide their historical studies for the following 14 years.

Lin's essay, "On the Principle Characteristics of Chinese Architecture," was a theoretical attempt to portray Chinese architecture, with its long evolution over thousands of years and strong influence across the vast Asian continent, as a unique and significant system. Moreover, Lin believed that China's wooden architecture demonstrated a profound construction system in which the pure timber frame structure was always incorporated with a coherent aesthetic expression. It was this principle of "structural rationalism" that rendered Chinese architecture equivalent to both the Gothic system in the West and the bourgeoning modernist architecture being constructed around the world. Lin further speculated about how traditional Chinese architecture could transform into a modern Chinese architecture. Since China's timber frame construction shared the same structural principles with modern reinforced concrete and steel frame construction, "one only needs to change the building materials, without radically changing the major structural parts, so that the possibility of the (new) materials will lead to a new development. That in turn will result in an extremely satisfying new architecture." [1]

Fully concurring with Lin's theoretical formulation of Chinese architecture, Liang's essay, "Architecture of the Tang Dynasty," offered a historical analysis that mapped out the evolution of Chinese architecture with a central thread that weaved together at least three separate strands of thinking. Following both Johann Joachim Winckelmann and Charles Darwin, he demonstrated how history evolved in a manner similar to life's cyclical growth: birth-adolescence-maturity-decline. This notion led to a nationalist conviction, shared by Liang and many other contemporary Chinese intellectuals, about the fate of Chinese culture. They argued that Chinese culture originated in ancient times, reached its peak during the Tang dynasty, gained its refinement during the Song dynasty, and started to decline during the Ming and Qing dynasties, leading finally to the early-twentieth-century reality that it was constantly being humiliated by encroaching Western cultures. Therefore, the writing of China's architectural history was of paramount importance to both Liang and Lin, as they believed that China's civilization could only be reconstructed through "the re-examination of its national heritage." [2]

Liang used a structural rationalist approach to show how "birth to decline" had been manifested in China's architectural history. In particular, he chose the evolution of wooden brackets as the most salient expression of the rise and fall of China's architectural culture. The configuration of the brackets from their early stage of simplicity, reached their complexity and maturity during the Tang and Song dynasties, and then gradually lost their structural value during the Ming and Qing dynasties, when they degenerated into mere decoration. Within this chronology, Liang believed that a high degree of prestige should be applied to Tang architecture because "Tang art was the golden moment of China's art history." [3] However, at the time, Liang was not certain that any examples of Tang construction had actually survived in China: he was only able to examine and admire Tang architecture by viewing the images of the Dunhuag Murals and photos of Hōryū-ji, a well preserved Tang temple in Nara, Japan.

Missing Components

Liang and Lin's historiographical construction was problematic in two respects. Firstly, they were so eager to portray China's traditional architecture as one singular *system*, as important as the Greek, Roman, and Gothic were in the West, that they overly generalized the concept of Chinese architecture. In their account, only one dominant architectural style could best represent China's national style: the timber structures exemplified by the Northern Chinese royal palaces and Buddhist temples, particularly the ones built during the period from the Tang to Jin dynasties. As a consequence of their idealization, the diversity of China's architectural culture—the multiple construction systems, building types, and vernacular buildings of different regions and ethnic groups—was omitted.

Secondly, Liang and Lin had theorized a concept of "Chinese architecture" before they had carried out a thorough, empirical study. In April 1932, one month after they published their two essays, Liang conducted his first field study in Ji County, Hebei. This was soon followed by more than 10 years of jointly conducted field research. Liang, Lin, and their colleagues painstakingly surveyed and documented each building and incorporated it into the historic, genealogical framework they had previously developed. In other words, each building became physical proof of their preconceived theory. Although Liang, Lin, and their colleagues have been credited as the first group of Chinese architectural scholars to emphasize the importance of research based on field studies, their approach was radically different from that of another contemporary historian, Fu Sinian, who insisted that historians should not follow or promote any "-ism", but should work with objective evidence only. Fu's famous slogan: "We're not intellectuals. We go all the way up to heaven and down to hell, with our hands and feet, to look for things." [4]

Climbing Up: 1932–1937

Between 1932 and 1937, Liang and Lin conducted numerous field trips to the countryside of Northern China to look for any remaining historical structures. Contrary to our common conception that one goes to the countryside to understand the vernacular, local, or low-end,

Liang and Lin went "down" in order to "climb up and trace back." In other words through documenting surviving canonical work in the countryside, they attempted to prove their projected chronology for their history of "Chinese architecture" and with it its apex; the golden moment of the Tang Dynasty.

Based on the knowledge they had gathered in Beijing reading about Ming and Qing architecture, they and their colleagues investigated a series of temples that had survived from the Yuan, Jin, Liao, and Tang dynasties. In July 1937, among numerous discoveries, their greatest triumph was the identification of the Foguang Temple in the Wutai Mountains, Shanxi Province: a timber structure dating back to 857 AD during the Tang Dynasty.

This breakthrough was a powerful repudiation of Japan's declaration that one could only see Tang structures in Japan, a position that had tormented Liang and Lin for years. Finding the Foguang Temple was the pinnacle of Liang and Lin's career.

Yet at this juncture, history could not have been more dramatic. The most glorious moment in Liang and Lin's career was also one of the darkest ones in China's modern history. On July 8, 1937, when Liang, Lin, and their colleagues were celebrating finding the Foguang Temple and were absorbed in measuring the building in the deep Wutai Mountains, the Lugouqiao Incident broke out on Beijing's outskirts, sparking the Second Sino-Japanese War. This forced Liang, Lin, and their colleagues to immediately flee to Southwest China, where they would stay in hiding for nine years.

Sent Down: 1937–1946

Despite its misery, the exile of Liang, Lin, and their colleagues to the Southwest ironically turned into a fruitful "grand tour" that greatly expanded their horizons.[5] Their escape across the continent opened their eyes to China's diverse building types, construction systems, and formal expressions in response to the variety of local material, climatic, and cultural conditions. Among all of their discoveries, vernacular housing opened up a new sphere of interest for their architectural study. During the period between 1932 and 1937, Liang and his colleagues focused exclusively on temples built according to royal construction standards and had been indifferent to vernacular housing, in spite of seeing examples everywhere during their trips to the countryside. Among the numerous study reports they published in the *Bulletin* during this period, not a single essay was devoted to these vernacular buildings. However, from the latter part of 1937 until 1946, their attitude changed dramatically.

Living in the remote countryside of Southwest China, they had to cope with the severe lack of financial support and access to transportation. Also, there were very few buildings constructed in accordance with the royal standard. Liang and his colleagues had no other choice but to closely study the humble buildings in which they resided or others that were nearby. For example, Liu Zhiping, an assistant of Liang, measured the courtyard house he inhabited in Kunming. He published a thorough report in the *Bulletin* in 1944, which was the first essay on China's vernacular housing ever written by a member of the Society for Research in Chinese Architecture.[6] Liu Dunzhen, Director of the Society's Literature Study Department and one of Liang's colleagues, measured his parents' countryside home, Liu Residence, in Hunan Province in 1944. Similarly, Liang also measured a courtyard compound in Li Zhuang, a small village on the outskirts of Chongqing, where they lived between 1944 and 1946.

Closure

Between 1932 and 1941, Liang and his colleagues visited more than 200 counties in 15 provinces and examined more than 2,000 traditional structures. Based on their case studies, Liang completed his manuscripts for the *History of Chinese Architecture* (in Chinese) in 1944 and *Chinese Architecture, A Pictorial History* (in English) in 1946.[7] Liang's two books were a full materialization of the intellectual blueprint that he and Lin had drawn up more than 10 years before. His *Pictorial History* was a direct expansion of the two essays he and Lin published in 1932 and focused only on the structural rationalist principles of Chinese timber construction and its evolution through four periods: Adolescence (CE, Han), Vigor (850–1050, Tang), Elegance (1000–1400, Song) and Rigidity (1400–1912, Ming and Qing). *History*, Liang's other book, did mention some other elements, such as masonry structures, vernacular housing, and gardens, but this section, compared to Liang's extensive account of timber royal palaces and temples, was quite marginal. The heterogeneous materials Liang and his colleagues collected during their exile in Southwest China, inclusive of: the vernacular, the minority, the ordinary, and the unorthodox, all of which could have added complexity and diversity to his historical account, were largely excluded or repressed in Liang's writing. Although Liang and Lin physically encountered the Chinese countryside, the countryside itself, whether it confirmed or challenged their prescribed trajectory of "Chinese architecture," never became an important issue.

Awareness of the countryside occurred 10 years later. During the 1950s, when Marxism/ Leninism became the dominant ideology in Mao's China, Liang was constantly attacked for being too bourgeois, with no sense of the class struggle. His colleague, Liu Dunzhen, one of the many who criticized Liang during this period, rose to prominence. All of the materials that Liang, Liu, and their colleagues had collected in Southwest China formed the central content of Liu's book, titled, *A Brief Account of Chinese Dwellings*, which was published in 1956.[8] However, such a "shift" was mainly forced onto Liu by the political context, rather than by the historian's own alternative thinking. Liu's book merely presented a picture catalogue of China's typical, vernacular houses rather than an historical study with new cultural insights.

For these historians working in this period, the countryside was simply not a vehicle for furthering their knowledge or definition of Chinese architectural history. It was not until the latter part of the twentieth century that China's architectural historians began to think of the countryside as a potential cultural counterpart against the orthodox conceptions of modernism, nationalism, and intellectual elitism.

(1) Lin Huiyin, "On the Principle Characteristics of Chinese Architecture," *Bulletin of the Society for Research in Chinese Architecture* Vol. III, No. 1 (1932), pg. 179.

(2) Liang and Lin were among the Chinese intellectuals who grew up during China's New Culture Movement of the mid 1910's and 1920s. They were particularly inspired by Hi Shi, one of movement's central leaders, who listed four major works that the Chinese intellectuals needed to carry out: "studying issues," "importing theories," "reexamining the national heritage" and "recreating civilization." Hu Shi, "The Meaning of New Tide," *New Youth* 7, No. 1, 1919.

(3) Liang Sicheng, "Architecture of the Tang Dynasty," *Bulletin* Vol. III, No. 1, 1932, pg. 114

(4) Fu Sinian, "The Objective of Working in the Institute of History and Philology," in: *Collection of Mr. Fu Mengzhen's Academic Essays*, Longmen Bookstore, Hong Kong 1969, pp. 179–180.

(5) On the way to the Southwest, Lin Huiyin was infected with tuberculosis, therefore much less involved in the field trips during the years of 1938–46.

(6) Liu Zhiping, "Yunnan Stamp House," *Bulletin* Vol. VII, No. 1, 1944, pp. 63–94.

(7) Liang's *History of Chinese Architecture* was formally published by Baihua Wenyi Publishing House (Tianjin) in 1998. His *Chinese Architecture, A Pictorial History* (in English), edited by Wilma Fairbank, was published by the MIT Press in 1984.

(8) Liu Dunzhen. *A Brief Account of Chinese Dwellings*, Beijing 1957.

▲ Mo Zhongjiang under the eaves of Ying County Wooden Tower, 1933.

▲ The Foguang Temple, 1937. Finding the Foguang Temple was the pinnacle of Liang and Lin's career.

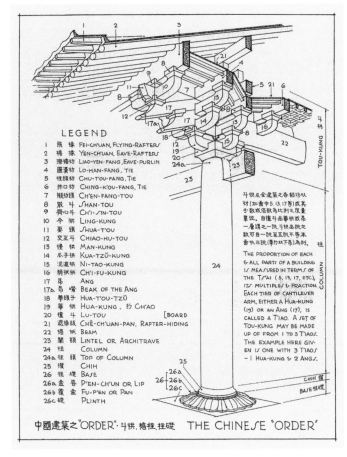

LEGEND

1 飛椽 FEI-CH'UAN, FLYING-RAFTERS
2 檐椽 YEN-CH'UAN, EAVE-RAFTERS
3 橑檐枋 LIAO-YEN-FANG, EAVE-PURLIN
4 羅漢枋 LO-HAN-FANG, TIE
5 柱頭枋 CHU-T'OU-FANG, TIE
6 井口枋 CHING-K'OU-FANG, TIE
7 襯枋頭 CH'EN-FANG-T'OU
8 散斗 SHAN-TOU
9 齊心斗 CH'I-SIN-TOU
10 令拱 LING-KUNG
11 耍頭 SHUA-T'OU
12 交互斗 CHIAO-HU-TOU
13 慢拱 MAN-KUNG
14 瓜子拱 KUA-TZŬ-KUNG
15 泥道拱 NI-TAO-KUNG
16 騎栿拱 CH'I-FU-KUNG
17 昂 ANG
17a 昂嘴 BEAK OF THE ANG
18 華頭子 HUA-T'OU-TZŬ
19 華拱 HUA-KUNG, 抄 CH'AO
20 櫨斗 LU-TOU
21 遮椽版 CHÊ-CH'UAN-PAN, RAFTER-HIDING [BOARD
22 搪栿 BEAM
23 闌額 LINTEL OR ARCHITRAVE
24 柱 COLUMN
24a 柱頭 TOP OF COLUMN
25 櫍 CHIH
26 柱礎 BASE
26a 盆唇 P'EN-CH'UN OR LIP
26b 覆盆 FU-P'EN OR PAN
26c 礎 PLINTH

斗拱及全建築之各部均以材(如图中5.13.17等)或其分數倍數為比例之度量單位. 自櫨斗出華拱或昂一層請之一跳, 斗拱出跳之數可自一跳至五跳不等本图以三跳(即功双下昂)為时.

THE PROPORTION OF EACH & ALL PARTS OF A BUILDING IS MEASURED IN TERMS OF THE TS'AI (5, 13, 17, ETC.), ITS MULTIPLES & FRACTION. EACH TIER OF CANTILEVER ARM, EITHER A HUA-KUNG (19) OR AN ANG (17), IS CALLED A T'IAO. A SET OF TOU-KUNG MAY BE MADE UP OF FROM 1 TO 5 T'IAOS. THE EXAMPLE HERE GIVEN IS ONE WITH 3 T'IAOS – 1 HUA-KUNG & 2 ANGS.

中國建築之"ORDER"·斗拱,搪柱,柱礎   THE CHINESE "ORDER"

◀ Liang's illustration of the Chinese "order" in his *Chinese Architecture, A Pictorial History*.

37

Mao Zedong and the Chinese Countryside

by Frank Dikötter

Let me start with a confession: I am not an architect. And if that wasn't bad enough, I don't really know much about the country-side either. That is not to say that I did not live in the countryside. When I was a boy, my village in Holland had about 120 households. But in my entire life, I never really met a farmer. I did see an occasional tractor in the fields at the edge of the village, but that's about it. Surrounding the village, there was a massive industrial complex called the Dutch State Mines, with beautiful cooling towers and massive slag heaps. As a little boy, peering through my window at night, I could see a sprawling petrolchemical complex with lights flickering throughout the night. That was what fired my imagination, not cows and cabbages.

When I was 12, my family moved to Switzerland and again, I was very lucky to live in the beautiful countryside surrounded by lush vineyards. My brother and I used to go scrumping for cherries and apples, like all other children.

By the time I went to China in 1985 as a student, it was pretty clear to me that the countryside is a place of beauty: "countryside equals good." But when I arrived, I was told that the equation was not exactly the same. My first experience with the countryside was when a friend and I decided to escape from Nankai University in Tianjin. In the middle of the night, we left for the beach resort of Beidaihe—it's about three days on a bicycle. We did this in the middle of the night because at that time in 1985, as a foreigner, you weren't allowed to leave the city. Large parts of the countryside were still fenced off. And for good reason, as we soon discovered: having to go through the night without any lights, avoiding all the potholes in the road, was a dangerous proposition. By the early hours of the morning we reached the port of Tanggu and veered north towards Tangshan. This city was destroyed in an ominous earthquake in 1976, as Mao was lying on his deathbed. For several hours, my friend and I cycled through rubbish. And I don't mean rubbish as a metaphor, I mean literally rubbish. A dump. Stuff dumped from the cities. We would occasionally encounter a farmer who was bringing a pig to market. Most of them were walking; a few were on bicycles. This went on for hours. First, I thought, "Well this is probably the exception, we just hit the biggest landfill on the planet," but over many decades, from 1985 till now, and on many trips back to China, I discovered a profound truth: the countryside is not a particularly nice place in the People's Republic of China. All too often it *is* a dump! There are places of great beauty, but overall it's not a very nice place. It's not entirely surprising that China is one of the few countries where people are desperate to get away from the countryside, even those who are wealthy. Typically, affluent people want to go from the city to the countryside! I have good reasons for why that is not the case in China, and that's what I want to talk about now.

People and places have histories. If there is one common mistake we make about China today, we tend to forget about history. It is understandable that the leaders in Beijing themselves are keen to forget about the first three decades of the People's Republic, as if China today somehow appeared out of nowhere. And the second mistake, when we look at history after 1949, is to skip the 1950s and go straight to the Cultural Revolution. Well, the Cultural Revolution starts roughly in the middle of the 1960s, but by that time the People's Republic has been around for good 15 years. That period is what I would like to focus on now, because it very much sets the tone. The majority of people lived in the countryside in 1949. My argument will be about what happened there from 1949 to 1962. The last four years of this period were marked by a horrific, manmade famine, sometimes referred to in communist propaganda as the Great Leap Forward. It is actually one of the greatest catastrophes in human history. At least 45 million people were worked or starved to death. Two to three million people were quite literally beaten to death, a few of them were buried alive. That is the history I would like to bring to your attention.

How does it all start? With liberation. And liberation in the countryside really means land reform. I hesitate to use the term *land reform*, because when you think about land reform it actually sounds pretty good. After all, Taiwan had land reform from roughly 1949 to 1952. At the same time, there was land reform in Japan and land reform in Korea. Nobody ever died in any of these three countries. But the so-called land reform in China was an extraordinarily bloody affair. Why was that? The conventional image we have is that Mao Zedong and the Communist Party somehow came and liberated the peasants (the term used to refer to farmers and villagers) from feudalism and the evil landlords who had exploited their labor for centuries. But now that the archives have opened up, there's an abundance of material to show that the story is in fact much more complex.

Most of the land reform started in Manchuria in 1946–47. Work teams were sent by the Communist Party to classify every single human being in the village according to a class status, ranking people as a landlord, a rich peasant, a middle peasant, a poor peasant, or a laborer based on a very clear hierarchy, where poor was considered good and rich was bad. They tried to impose a very rigid system on these villagers, one which did not really correspond to the social landscape of Manchuria, let alone the rest of the extraordinary diversity of the countryside in China. The reality was that in most of these Manchurian villages, most of the farmers were pretty much the same: there were very few landlords. In Yuanbao, one of the villages where land reform started, the man who was described as a landlord had two window panes in his mud hut. The other villagers also had mud huts, but they didn't have two glass window panes. That was the difference between being poor and being rich.

The work teams who were sent to analyze these villagers spent many evenings for weeks and weeks trying to win over the majority of people who they would classify as poor peasants. They tried to change small, petty grievances into something more systematic called class hatred. And they did so very patiently. They were quite literally making a revolution by building it up from the bottom, by turning loosely knit villages into a majority pitted against the traditional power holders. And they tried to do this by saying that accounts should be settled. People classified as landlords, they claimed, had exploited the majority of peasants for centuries, and now these peasants should demand compensation. The land of these victims, as well as all of their possessions, were promised to the peasants.

Gradually the military arrived, sealed off these villages, and rallies were organized. Victims were paraded through the villages and brought onto platforms where they were beaten to death. Few people had a choice: if they refused to denounce the landlords during these mass rallies, they themselves could become victims, accused of sheltering landlords. In some places up to 10% of all villagers were killed. Their land was redistributed, their belongings were taken. There is one man from Yuanbao, still alive today, who remembers that he received a water jug. There's another farmer who remembers that he got a horse's leg. Because one of the victims they killed had a horse, they shared the horse among four families: each one of them got a leg. It was part of the victory for having strangled this landlord to death.

So what really was land reform? First of all, it was a way for the Communist Party to get most of the farmers to bloody their hands. It was a pact between the majority of poor people sealed in the blood of a minority. And once this majority of villagers had bloodied their hands, they no longer had anybody to turn to for protection, except the Communist Party of China. There's a proverb in Chinese: "The poor rely on the rich, the rich rely on heaven." Once you eliminate the rich, nobody has anyone to rely on but the Communist Party of China. Once they had their hands bloodied, these villagers feared the return of the old regime, and so to make sure that the old regime would not come back, some of the young men joined the People's Liberation Army.

There is something else. Before land reform, the greatest asset in China—from the small villages in Manchuria with individual households to the large, sprawling clans in Guangdong—was the land. And farmers in closely knit villages would keep a good portion of the land hidden from tax collectors. But now that the land had been distributed and the Party had surveyed it, the party was in a position to tax everybody. Everybody who got

a share of the land would now have to pay a certain amount of tax in grain to feed the People's Liberation Army. As you can tell, land reform was a bloody affair. There are places where people were stripped of their clothes, frozen during the winter, or buried alive. Frequently, the targets who the party singled out were tortured. As they had been identified as landlords, they were supposed to have gold, money, or jewels. Only pain would force them to reveal where they had hidden these assets. As Mao Zedong said: "Revolution is no dinner party!"

You might think that with liberation, a more equitable distribution of the land would cause the economy to soar ahead. But this did not quite happen. Since everybody had a roughly similar plot of land and since everybody had to pay tax to the Party in the form of grain, small private entrepreneurship rapidly declined—including sideline occupations that traditionally kept farmers busy for a good part of their working days. For instance, entire villages specialized in making umbrellas or soles for cotton shoes. These activities were curbed, partly because the Party viewed them with suspicion, but also because the Party gave a much higher priority to the production of grain. Everybody was sent to the countryside to work the land. But they didn't have tools, they didn't have animals. Remember that horse I mentioned earlier, divided by four families? Where do you get a horse to plough the fields if you slaughter it first?

So the next stage on the road to collectivization is mutual-aid teams. Farmers are told to share their tools and pool their cattle. I don't know about you, but personally I don't really like to share much. If you think that the farmers are any different, you should think again. If you are a farmer and you still have some tools left, despite the violence of land reform, and your neighbor would like to borrow these tools, the chances are pretty high that you will worry that he won't take care of your prized possessions, particularly if your neighbor is a Party activist with more power than you. The mutual-aid teams are part of a gradual process of impoverishment. The revolution produced an environment in which it is dangerous to be rich or successful. One of the slogans at the time is that it is "glorious to be poor." To be even moderately rich means that one is in danger of being seen as a landlord or rich peasant. With the mutual-aid teams comes huge resistance. "Why would I share my ducks?" some farmers wonder. "I would rather slaughter them and eat them." "Why would I share my tools?"—"I would rather destroy them!" Waves of destruction ripple through the countryside as a result.

In 1953 the party decided to make sharing even more permanent, creating cooperatives that pooled together ever-greater number of villagers. But most of all, the state imposed a monopoly on the grain that very same year. For centuries farmers had decided what they wanted to grow and where they wanted to sell it. Now they had to produce grain—millet, potatoes, rice—and sell it to the state at state-mandated prices. Not only that, but the state also dictated that all the grain above a certain threshold had to be sold. In other words, the farmers were only allowed to keep a very small portion of what they produced to feed themselves. That threshold actually corresponded to a starvation diet. The monopoly on grain in effect left farmers with barely enough grain to get through the year. The rest was taken away by the state to feed the cities, to buy equipment from the Soviet Union, and to build up industries.

More restrictions came in 1955. Despite the monopoly on grain, the party was not satisfied. It wanted to be able to move the grain straight from the fields into state granaries. So high-level cooperatives were introduced, followed by state collectives. This meant that the land was taken away from the villagers to become state property. The farmers lost their plots. Not only that, in 1955, the state also introduced a household registration system (*hukou*). It was equivalent to an internal passport system. It meant that every person was registered in his place of origin, and the system made a huge difference between those registered as city dwellers and those registered as peasants. Access to food, education, and social services was all determined by the household registration system, which also curbed freedom of movement. In other words, farmers could no longer seek work in the cities and were given an inferior social status. Up until 1949, and to some extent up to 1955, villagers could leave the countryside to look for better opportunities or to flee from famine. Now they were tied to the land, even though the land no longer belonged to them.

By 1956, villagers were quite literally serfs: bonded servants of the state. They had no land, no control over their crops, no control over their work schedules, and they no longer had freedom of movement. They were made to work under the orders of local party cadres. Now you might think that this was bad enough, but it got a lot worse. For reasons which are too complex to explain in this article, Mao Zedong launched the Great Leap Forward in 1958. The immediate reason is that he was impatient and wished to increase production. He wanted to overtake the Soviet Union. After Stalin's death in 1953, Khrushchev took over the leadership of the communist camp. In 1957, at a meeting of all the leaders of socialist countries in Moscow, he boldly announced that the Soviet Union would overtake the United States in the production of butter and milk. Mao Zedong, who was a guest at the meeting, saw it as a challenge and announced to the world that if the Soviet Union was going to overtake the United States in the production of butter, China would, within 15 years, overtake the United Kingdom in the production of steel. How was he going to do this? He had a very powerful vision. Taking the land away from the farmers was not quite enough. Making sure that the grain went straight from the fields to the state granaries was not quite sufficient either. He believed that the real wealth of China was in the hundreds of millions of peasants. If only he could organize them like an army, if only he could deploy them in one wave after another in a continuous revolution, tackling water conservancy projects during the slack winter months, producing iron in backyard furnaces during the summer, increasing the grain crop in tightly organized battalions, then surely China could cross the golden bridge from socialism to communism.

In 1958 hundreds of millions of farmers were herded into giant people's communes. At this stage they lost everything. We know what happened. From 1958 to 1962, tens of millions of people were starved, worked, or beaten to death. Why? Because the cadres on the ground had to whip up the workforce in one drive after another. And few of them really cared for that workforce, as they were under pressure to produce results. Many treated the villagers like livestock. People had to be housed, they had to be clothed and they had to be fed, and all of that came at a cost to the state. It was very tempting for the local cadres to treat people not so much as people but like mere tools. Here was already a planned economy that reduced people to mere digits on paper. The state was everything, the individual nothing. One's worth was constantly assessed through work points, by the ability to plant rice or dig earth. So the temptation was to cut off from the food supply those people who simply couldn't work hard enough. With

all the grain taken away by the state from the countryside, it was already difficult enough to feed good workers, let alone those who were too old, or too weak, or too sick to contribute to the regime through their labor. There was not enough food to go around. People had to queue up at the canteen, where local cadres started to use food as a weapon. They punished people who spoke out or did not work hard enough by banning them from the canteen—quite literally starving them to death. Sometimes deprivation of food was not considered to be harsh enough, so some farmers who resisted collectivization and the Great Leap Forward were beaten with sticks, or made to work in the middle of the winter without any clothes.

By the end of 1962, the countryside was a broken place, a place where people were being forced by widespread famine to do horrendous things to each other just in order to stay alive. It was a place ruled by fear. Entire villages had been wiped off the map. In some regions a quarter of the population died, generally old people, women, and children. The countryside had become a place of extraordinary brutality, not only brutality against fellow human beings but also against nature. All over China people were made to dig earth and to build reservoirs and dams, for instance. Frequently, a lot of that work led to massive damage, causing landslides, river silting, soil salinization, and devastating floods. When these farmers were made to produce steel in backyard furnaces in 1958, they would go to the forest and cut down the trees for fuel—but later they went back go to cut even more down, just to stay warm and alive. There are provinces in China where up to half of the forest disappeared.

Since we are all here to talk about architecture, it's important to understand that housing was also devastated. In Hunan Province Liu

Shaoqi himself wrote a report that stated that 40% of all housing has vanished. Why? For all sorts of reasons. At first houses were torn down to make fertilizer. In some cases this did make sense. If you take a small hut in which cows have lived for a long time, the mud walls will contain some organic matter and these walls can be ground down to powder and strewn across the fields. But before long, people were forced to contribute to the movement to increase fertilizer supply. So entire houses were torn down. And sometimes houses were destroyed as a form of punishment. If you refused to pay tax or deliver the grain, the militia would come and take away your door, your roof, your house, everything. If you were suspected of hiding grain, they would come and try to find it behind the walls or under the floor. Another reason is that some of the local cadres believed the propaganda and could see a socialist utopia beckoning ahead, so they started destroying all the houses, thinking that they would build something far more beautiful. But the plan never managed to migrate from paper to the ground. So the houses were torn down and nothing was built in their place. People also cannibalized their own houses. They literally ate the plaster from the walls. I remember an interview with an old woman who explained that as a young girl, in 1961, she started to eat the thatch of her roof. She was so starved that she thought that it tasted really delicious. As a result there were places where up to families had to share one small hut. Tens of millions of people did not have a roof over their heads at all. By 1962 the Chinese countryside was a place of ruin.

How about the following decades? Until Mao's death in 1976 very little changed, although there was no longer mass starvation. The people's communes remained in place and villagers remained servants of the state. And some of the structures of inequality that

date from the Maoist era have survived to this day, such as the household registration system. To this day, people from the countryside are considered to be second-rank citizens in China, legally and otherwise. So when you go to a village in the People's Republic—as a scholar, as an architect, as a tourist—bear in mind that most of the villagers have not had much of a voice since 1949. But it does not mean that they don't have extraordinarily tragic and complex histories.

This article is an edited transcript from the Homecoming Symposium, April 13, 2012.

▲ Zhang Yuqing, *Fenfa Tuqiang Gaizao Ziran*: "Go all out to make the country strong and remake nature," 1965, propaganda poster.

▲ Chen Yanning, *Mao Zhuxi Shicha Guangdong Nongcun*: "Chairman Mao inspects a village in Guangdong," 1972, propaganda poster.

Pining for the Native Soil

by Robin Visser

In the late 1980s, I spent my first two years in China in an economic management cadres college in rural Xixiang Tang on the outskirts of Nanning, the capital of Guangxi, an autonomous Zhuang minority region bordering Vietnam in the subtropics. From the top deck of my two-story cottage I would sip tea and watch the local farmers plowing the fields with their oxen, a timeless scene that, aside from the industrial waste gradually filling the river, was replicated for hundreds of years. To break the lulling rhythms of organic rural life, my American colleague and I would cycle the one hour into the city to enjoy the southern "nightlife"— eating from outdoor food stalls and purchasing odds and ends from the private peddlers who began to proliferate city streets in the mid-1980s. Other than the occasional Zhang Yimou movie, screened to packed crowds who carried their own chairs and umbrellas to the outdoor theater (the college basketball court) surrounded by banyan trees, our major forms of entertainment were work-unit sponsored ballroom dances or the new karaoke bars just starting to spring up. China wasn't exactly known for its urban stimulation in the 1980s; adventure was found by roaming the vast countryside exploring China's scenery, ethnic customs, and historical artifacts.

As urbanization intensified throughout the 1990s, I witnessed radical changes to formerly rural landscapes. In 1993 I found the sleepy cadres college in Xixiang Tang surrounded by high-class Cantonese restaurants, hotels, karaoke bars, and discos.

The quiet path to a secluded swimming reservoir dotted with small islands, where I often cycled with my students through acres of green rice paddies, was now a paved cacophonous road that assaulted the senses with gaudy buildings, plastic watertoys, hawkers, and Cantopop. The unassuming fishing village of Beihai had become peppered with high-rise resort hotels, with tourists arriving daily on direct flights from Hong Kong and via a new highway from Nanning. From the western cities of Xining, Lanzhou, Xian, Wuhan, to seaside cities such as Qingdao and Sanya, urban expansion steadily engulfed China's countryside, swiftly cementing over its cultural roots.

A nation on the move, the Chinese cultural psychology has become, for many, one of perpetual homelessness, an uncanny sense of *unheimlich*. China's unprecedented speed of destruction and building gives new urgency to the human need to imagine, and experience, places of origin. A homecoming is in order. Gaston Bachelard speaks eloquently to the universal attachment to the childhood home in *The Poetics of Space* (1994), yet how does one come home? It is not coincidental that Y. C. James Yen (1893–1990) was inspired to launch China's rural reconstruction movements after helping illiterate Chinese workers in post-First World War France write letters to their home villages. According to the eminent sociologist Fei Xiaotong (1910–2005), a longing for home historically organized Chinese society. In *From the Soil: The Foundations of Chinese Culture* (1992; *Xiangtu Zhongguo*, 1947) he locates the intense Chinese attachment to the village home in its land-bound, agrarian roots of culture. In *Rural Reconstruction* (*Xiangtu Chongjian*, 1948), he details how Chinese society, whether in the countryside or the city, is unified by the notion of ties to native soil. Artist-activist Ou Ning, founder of Bishan Commune, a group of intellectuals devoted to rural reconstruction, describes it in this way:

"Before so-called modernization, China's country-side provided the cities with children who would grow into the next generation of elites, and form associations in the cities with others from the same hometowns. Longing for their hometowns, these city dwellers would often send money back to the countryside, and thus supported rural areas with the construction of ancestral temples and schools, or aid for the poor and orphans." [1]

Today, small groups of Chinese intellectuals, increasing numbers of middle-class urbanites, along with rural residents, are revitalizing the rural reconstruction movement to resist intensive rural development. They cultivate the political, economic, and cultural resources of rural areas, actively promoting local imperatives to counter neoliberal globalization. Such localized resistance is necessary to counter China's twenty-first-century strategy of land development, which has escalated to the scale of regional (sub)urbanization planning, usurping quaint twentieth-century notions of urban planning. Under the banner of its current policy of regional "urban-rural integration," China now leads what might be called the worldwide "suburbanization revolution." Given China's two-tiered land system, where most of China's urban land is owned by the state and most rural land is owned by village collectives, entrepreneurial local governments and institutions leverage their power to convert farmlands to con-structed lands for industrial and commercial development. The motivation for most development projects, whether urban or rural, lies in their speculative value rather than delivering a social or ecological good.

In 2012 I traveled throughout Xinjiang Province, interviewing local poets and writers while documenting destruction of the grasslands north of Shihezi, demolition of the ancient city of Kashgar, and the massive state-funded industrial projects along the snow-capped mountains on the Karakoram Highway to Pakistan. For the writers, and many residents whom I interviewed, it is the land that provides a sense of security, of home. When asked what she most liked about Xinjiang, the writer Li Juan answered:

"What I like most about Xinjiang is that my home is here. I don't like to stray too far from home. The land here is very desolate and barren, the ecology is extremely fragile, the people live very difficult lives ... Only those people who are creative, who have the right attitude, will be able to survive here ... So the arts that it does produce are always so powerful and fervent, so wide open and tolerant but also having a sadness to them ... It's a joyous, celebratory sadness." [2]

My Shanghainese mother-in-law, visiting us in Chapel Hill, cried in gratitude when she read Li Juan's nature essays on Altay, in eastern Xinjiang, a place she had never visited. Li Juan's intimacy with the land, with home, evoked a powerfully joyous, celebratory sadness in that Chinese woman, in this American woman, pining for the native soil.

(1)   "Bishan Project: Restarting the Rural Reconstruction Movement." (6 April 2013). Ou Ning's blog: http://www.alternativearchive.com/ouning/article.asp?id=897 (accessed 13 May 2013).
(2)   Ou Ning introduced me to Li Juan's essays, collected in *My Altay*.

▲ A Sense of
Home. Hongcun
Village, Anhui
Province, 2006.

◀ Luo Zhongli,
Father, 1980,
oil on canvas,
221×155 cm.
Collection
National Art
Museum of China.

In the Name of the Father

Thinking the Rural in Contemporary Chinese Art

by Philip Tinari

If you go to the National Art Museum of China around any major state, party, or institutional anniversary, the wrinkled, toothless face of Luo Zhongli's *Father* will be there to greet you. Painted in a hyperrealist mode that has been said to result from an early encounter with reproductions of work by Chuck Close, the iconic canvas turns a monumental lens on a subject remarkable mainly for its ordinariness, a directional move that had previously been used for the Chairman alone. Completed in 1980, this forthright depiction of a peasant hero marks the high point of one of the founding currents in contemporary art in China: the "native soil" movement, with its down-home emphasis on the goodness of farmers, a posture that differed slightly but absolutely from an orthodox Maoist insistence on the intellectual's capacity to learn from them. "The idea for my painting," Luo Zhongli has written, "emerged from the moment I saw a peasant standing guard over nightsoil" by a public toilet near Chongqing.[1]

The surface still shines with the oily glow of many paintings from that era, and the pigment clumps in ways that are not apparent from the infinite reproductions that circulate in China. It is a massive canvas (221 × 155 cm), large explains Luo because "only as such, in front of this enormous head, can I feel the pressure from his kind, ox- or sheep-like eyes, hear his heavy breathing, see his pulsing veins and his racing bloodstream, smell the odor of tobacco and sweat, and feel his skin trembling with beads oozing from his pores."[2] Behind the figure's left ear there famously sits a pen, perhaps added to lend an air of optimism to what might otherwise be seen as a harrowing depiction of a long, bitter life. Luo Zhongli, for his part, saw things otherwise. "This is indeed the father who birthed and nurtured me. Standing in front of such a humble, kind, and hardworking father, who cannot but be moved?" he asked, shortly after the painting was first published.[3]

Fast forward to 2009. Luo Zhongli has made a successful career for himself in his native Sichuan, parlaying the fame first won with this painting into artistic renown and administrative power. His particular breed of experimental, though ultimately palatable painting, combined with its stance of earnest respect for the labor of the Chinese masses, has weathered particularly well through decades of reform. He holds a high position in the China Artists Association and the directorship of the Sichuan Fine Arts Institute, his alma mater and that of many other painters who now enjoy incomes and reputations far beyond anything they might have anticipated as students. There is a well-known scholarship named in his honor—a prize for young artists about to graduate from any of the country's art academies—and I have been invited to Chongqing to serve on the jury.

After we have convened and made our selections, I am driven by a faculty member from the area of Huangjiaoping—a dock-and-factory neighborhood on a bluff above the Yangtze, home to what was once "Asia's largest smokestack" and for years the gritty turf on which aspiring artists studying at the academy came face-to-face with the realities of an industrial economy—to "University Town" on the city's far rural fringes. It is an hour-long trek over new highways and bridges, past clusters of yet uninhabited apartment blocks, through freshly dug tunnels, alongside light-rail lines not yet completed—in short the sort of journey one often made in China during the late 2000s. We arrive in University Town and enter the new campus of the Sichuan Fine Arts Institute, to which the undergraduates have all just been moved. As a campus it feels immediately different from the normal flat, walled grid: Director Luo has decided to leave the plot's original topography intact, rather than bulldoze the trees and hills. The classrooms, studios, and faculty housing peek out from behind vegetation that seems only slightly manicured, offering students ample opportunities for "sketching from life" (*xiesheng*), that staple of art education in China, without even having to leave campus. At the heart of the complex there remains a single peasant household, residing in the same wooden dwelling it had inhabited before the surrounding land was zoned for demolition, tasked now with cultivating vegetables for consumption in the school's cafeteria, and with modeling, consciously or inadvertently, for the students. "This is just how Director Luo wanted things," the young professor explains to me. "Even after all these years and all this success, he still believes in the wisdom of the peasants."

I remember the extreme confusion I felt at the conclusion of this visit, a walkaround past libraries, printmaking studios, and dormitories. Exactly where on the (admittedly imperfect) continuum of authenticity to artifice should such an environment be placed? How to understand the overlapping, partial discourses that have structured its look and feel: environmental sustainability, educational excellence, technocratically mandated development, the primacy of encounter with an authentic peasant other, and most bafflingly, the idea of providing that rural encounter with the same corporate efficiency used by American universities to service their students? Add to this the fact that a huge percentage of students at any given Chinese university themselves come from rural families, and the semiotic layering on display in this new campus comes to seem stranger still. Back in Beijing, upon hearing of my trip, friends who belong to the last few classes to have graduated from the original campus of the Sichuan Institute voiced their disdain. "Out there in University Town, the students actually talk about how to become president of the student union," one remarked. From the perspective of artists who had cut their teeth on the social tensions so readily apparent back in Huangjiaoping, University Town looked like a velvet prison, where artists, placed in a setting that could be more or less contained, were left to focus on the sorts of things—career advancement, basic romance—that students of management or foreign language at the other nearby universities were supposed to care about. To others inside the Institute, it seems like an administrative folly—a debt-heavy project prodded along by easy access to financing under the bygone Bo Xilai regime. In any case, the campus stands, five years into its existence, as a unique sublimation of Luo Zhongli's very particular, and somehow very compelling, ideas about the importance of an abstracted rural consciousness as a wellspring for artistic and cultural practice in contemporary China.

This understanding of the rural is but one of several in play in the Chinese cultural sphere these days. At another end of the spectrum, about a year ago, Ou Ning relocated to Bishan, a small village in southern Anhui Province. To the Beijing art world, this came as something of a shock: long at the forefront of the conversation on contemporary Chinese art, design, and literature, Ou Ning is about as close to the ideal of an urban intellectual as one can get. His engagements have spanned everything from state-run art and architecture biennales to underground films about contested demolitions. He was one of the first people in the art world to maintain a regular blog, and his online presence remains vast. But after a few years of contemplation, he decided to leave Beijing, where he had moved from Guangzhou about a decade earlier, and settle in Bishan.

Ou Ning's take on rural reconstruction—a discourse that reaches far beyond the spheres of art and culture—hinges on the notion that humanistic practice can become a catalyst for social change. Specifically, he sees the sort of substantive activities he and his cohort might organize as an antidote to a more rote mode of development in which the surrounding villages, renowned for their natural and architectural beauty, have begun charging ticket fees. "The key issues of the countryside are not cultural," he has written, "but economic. Thus, although our work has set off on cultural terms, we'd still like to be able to implement it economically…as more [cultural practitioners] move in, after a while bookshops, restaurants will appear, and a local economy will slowly and organically form. If we can make Bishan popular, then the ticketing regulations of the popular nearby villages will be automatically annulled."[4]

His is a vision that comes across as new in a Chinese context, where interventions into the rural have not been known for this sort of compassion and sophistication. For so many Chinese artists, art has been a way to leave the countryside and become urban; the idea of art as a pretext for a return to the rural has not really taken root. The artistic trajectory from city back to countryside is a well-established modality in contexts like the United States—just think of Mass MoCA in North Adams, Massachusetts; Dia: Beacon in New York; the artist colony of Skowhegan; the mythology around Black Mountain College in the postwar years; or the current nexus around Marfa, Texas. These sorts of initiatives have not yet sprung from the Chinese art scene, which, we must remember, has only been institutionally articulated and politically sanctioned for about a decade. The trend has rather been for cities throughout the country to build museums and redevelop industrial precincts into art districts, on ever more massive and elaborate scales, albeit with little relation to their often newly hatched contexts. Seen in this light, Ou Ning's decision to home in on a small village in Anhui in an effort to create an alternative center of gravity for artistic happenings comes to seem prescient.

For Ou Ning this engagement has not been without its perils. A large portion of the festival that he and his collaborators had organized for fall 2012 was barred from opening amidst the generally tense atmosphere that preceded the Eighteenth Party Congress. For a practitioner looking to work seriously in a local, rural context, these micropolitics are paramount. As Ou Ning has written, "First we have to change the government and the people's view of us: if they want something done, then we do it. That way we'll gradually win their approval, and once they start to believe that we really have the capabilities to improve the area economically, then we can start to focus on the things we want to do, including our more political, 'anarchist' experiments."[5] What these might be, and how they might relate to future artistic and cultural developments, remains unclear. For now, the idea, and ideal, of a culturally driven rural concentration, at once deeply local and internationally networked, mindful of its immediate surroundings but with an ambition to transform rural consciousness through advanced cultural practice, seems replete with possibility for a scene at constant risk of subsumption by market, ideological, and stylistic squabbles. Perhaps a stream of exhibitions, talks, and screenings will turn this town around. More likely, those who come from beyond to participate in them will find, as Luo Zhongli did in the late 1970s and as he hopes his students might again today, an honest reality in the day-to-day life of the village.

▶ Chu Di Fang performance at the Bishan Harvestival, July 2011.

▼ Exhibition opening at the Bishan Harvestival, July 2011.

(1)   Luo Zhongli, "A Letter from the Artist of *Father* (Wo de Fuqin de zuozhe de laixin)," *Meishu* vol. 158, no. 2, 1981, pp. 4–5. Reproduced in Wu Hung, ed. *Chinese Contemporary Art: Primary Documents*, pg. 24, Translated by Michelle Wang.
(2)   Ibid.
(3)   Ibid., pg. 25.
(4)   Ou Ning, "Obstacles to Rural Reconstruction," *LEAP* 17 (October 2012).
(5)   Ibid.

B

Materializing the Rural

The global supply of construction materials, hasty construction, and default techniques has produced, in the past two decades, indiscriminating architectures in the urban centers and rural regions of China. Contrary to this process the architects in Materializing the Rural are experimenting with a language of architecture that revolves around the application and technique of materials and construction. Responding to the local environment, economy, culture, and history, site-specific projects are discussed in relation to vernacular construction intelligence and the architects' modern design sensibilities.

The Great Experiment Forward[1]

Position by Juan Du

Rapid development brought on by three decades of policy reforms has turned China into a global economic powerhouse. Since the radical reforms initiated in the late 1970s and early 1980s by Premier Deng Xiaoping, planned urbanization and a market economy have drastically altered China's political and social landscape. Beyond abstract statistics of GDP and capital gain, the sheer amount of matter produced and consumed in the process of urbanization is a more visceral indication of the scale and pace of this great experiment forward. China has become the world's leading consumer of construction materials such as steel, concrete, and timber. Demand for raw steel in 2013 is estimated to be 700 million tons, roughly half of the global supply. Along with astounding economic indicators of progress, also arisen are unprecedented air pollution, water shortage, and immense disparity between the country's urban centers and rural villages. In the global interest of China's developmental ascent, often overlooked is the social and environmental impact of China's urbanization process on the country's vast rural regions.

To carry out the experiment of "capitalism with socialist character," China's urban and industrial centers required a cheap labor force. One of the most daring political risks taken by Deng's government was allowing the rural population to work in cities, thereby loosening the rural-urban divide as characterized by the Mao era. In parallel with natural resources, human capital is the tangible material of China's urbanization. Nearly one-third of China's 200 million migrant workers are employed by the construction industry: it is a rural labor force that has built urban China.

While China's government has enjoyed the limelight brought on by the country's development and increasing economic power, it has also come to realize the current model will not be sustainable. During the 2013 National People's Congress, the central government very publicly recognized the vast environmental problems, social inequities, and urban-rural disparity resulting from the vast scale and rapid speed of development. However, as announced during the congress, planned urbanization will continue and even take on a more prominent role as the most important economic development tool to keep up with the great expectations of extraordinary growth. This drive for continued urbanization is placing increasing pressure on the rural regions as urban areas are running out of cheap land for development, thereby threatening the country's arable landscape.

The following section presents architectural responses that extract ideas from their rural contexts, materializing them into meaningful reflections on the evolving condition of China's countryside. Working with local communities, these projects not only are imbued with the wisdoms of their respective region's cultural heritage and traditional craft, but also aim to contribute to their sites' cultural and economic development through inventive and contemporary architectural approaches. The Museum of Handicraft Paper, located in Yunnan's Xinzhuang Village and designed by Hua Li, was built with local materials and through an intimate working relationship with the village builders, and aimed to contribute to the long-term development of the village. Wang Weijen explores and tests different applications of the Chinese courtyard typology according to different programs, scales and sites. With the House for All Seasons in Shaanxi's Shijia Village, John Lin aims to create a flexible prototype that provides the village with an alternative direction of rural development. Zhang Ke's Village Mountains and Rice Field Skyscrapers are utopic provocations calling attention to the depletion of the country's agricultural land. Liu Jiakun's Rebirth Brick projects and Memorial for Huishan poignantly demonstrate how architecture must become an active participant and advocate in re-establishing the processes and values of society. Perhaps not uncoincidentally, the project's initial techniques of utilizing post-earthquake debris found continued usage in taking in the waste materials generated through waves of destructive demolition linked to large-scale construction.

Relentless developmental pressures and hasty operations have produced indiscriminating architectures in the urban centers and rural regions throughout China. The building industry and architectural profession in general have played a key role in facilitating this situation. Architecture has never been simply about production of form or demonstration of technologies. Each era's creation serves to reflect the culture and ethics of the times. Future generations will judge our current values based on the physical artifacts we leave behind. China and the rest of the world need to find new models of development that are more environmentally and socially responsible for both urban and rural regions. Otherwise, when the construction dust settles, home will not be a welcome place for return.

---

(1) The title alludes to the Great Leap Forward, a late 1950s modernization campaign in China that ended catastrophically due to many reasons, one of which being the overzealous and poorly planned nationwide capital construction projects. Devastation and human suffering were most evident in the rural countryside. The allusion expresses this author's premonition over the possibility of the current Chinese experiment becoming another Great Leap Forward if historical lessons are unlearned.

◀ Key characters
of the project:
my friends, a
scholar (left) and
a graphic designer
(right), with
Long Zhanxian
(back), the head
of the village and
a master of
paper-making, and
Long Zhanwen
(middle), the main
builder and master
carpenter of
the village.

Tracing the Roots

Museum of Handicraft Paper

by Hua Li

The Museum of Handicraft Paper is situated in a remote village close to Tengchong in southwest Yunnan Province. The village has a very long tradition of paper-making and lies in a valley on the west side of the Gaoligong Mountains.

The key characters of this project are my friends: one is a scholar interested in traditional cultural research in remote areas in China and the other is a graphic designer. Our original intention was to invest in this village to develop it alongside preserving the paper-making tradition. Long Zhanxian, the head of the village and a master of paper-making, and Long Zhanwen, the main builder and master carpenter, were the important key characters from the village side.

The paper-making is done with a screen and mostly by hand. The material comes from the local *gou shu pi* (mulberry tree bark). The paper-makers soften the grind to make the pulp, filter it, and produce the paper. Unfortunately, in these times, the use of this paper product is declining. The paper-making tradition is in danger of losing its means, as it is only used for tea packaging or for traditional paper printing.

The original proposal from Long Zhanxian, the village head, for this project was to relocate or buy an old house in the village to transform it into a museum. I persuaded my friends to build a contemporary house, or museum, to show the process of paper-making.

We hope that the museum is not just a building, but becomes part of the sustainable development of the village. And we hope that we can continue to be part of that process.

Before we started to work on the design we investigated the local materials and building methods. We consulted Long Zhanwen, our builder and master carpenter, about the available materials and also their cost. This was quite important because this project had a very small budget. The typical vernacular architecture in that region is built in timber with a masonry enclosure either by adobe brick or regular brick.

The first model we made for the design was done without a site plan. We used only our memory and photos to produce a series of studies. The basic idea for the design was the micro-village. We made a cluster of smaller buildings to enable an appropriate dialogue with the existing village. Various galleries show the different processes of paper-making.

We built many models as a communication tool with the local builders. Local builders don't read construction drawings. The builders are used to drawing on cardboard, whereas we brought computers and models. The model is definitely the most efficient way to communicate the building idea. We built structural models and study models with details on how to construct the building. On site we even built, together with the local builders, a 1:6 model. That's their typical way of understanding the idea of the space and the tectonic system. Once they build the model, they can start the construction.

◄ Traditional village house in Yunnan built with the traditional nail-less mortise and tenon (*sun mao*) joint system.

▲ The traditional paper-making process and tools.

◄ I found this object in the village. It is a board the villagers use to cut tobacco. It is inspirational because the shape and the texture records what has happened to this object. It traces time and information.

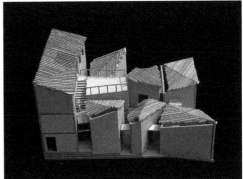

▲ The cluster
design of the
museum enables
an appropriate
dialogue with the
existing village.

◀ ▼ Study and
structure models
built during the
design process.

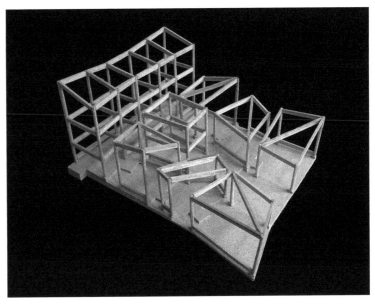

The structure uses the traditional nail-less mortise and tenon *(sun mao)* joint system. Although the form of the museum is modern, we used local bamboo for the roof and the wall finish is made of the paper they fabricate in the village. We even designed the furniture from bamboo.

With the opening ceremony of the construction process—a local tradition—the builders built the foundation and assembled the structural frame on the ground. They then used a machine to raise it. Long Zhanwen told me he saves labor with this machine. Before, 50 people had to work on a construction like this, but now he only needs seven or eight.

Raising the structure was very fast and very intelligent, because the builders used the trees on site as scaffolding. When the structure was finished, Long Zhanwen—he is really a master—cut one beam, which was too long, directly in the air without disassembling the building. Just like we would do it with the model. I was amazed!

These local builders are really efficient and skillful in doing timber construction, but once we encountered technical issues that they were not familiar with, it created problems. For example: with the waterproofing of the stone we used. This stone is local, but it is porous and absorbs a lot of moisture. To waterproof the stone we had to coat it with a sealant. However, the local builders had never done this before, so we had to experiment with transparent paint, which took a lot of time and trial-and-error testing.

Last year the government had built a new road from Tengchong to this area. A lot of old houses had to be torn down due to the expansion of the road, including Long Zhanwen's—the builder's—home. But because his house is built with a timber system, he simply disassembled and rebuilt the house on a new site assigned to him. I understand this as a recycling process. For me the traditional timber construction responds to the situation in China, as the land is always being redistributed due to our changing land policies. However, at the same time that this road was being built, the whole region was starting to transform through using industrial materials and building techniques. Recently, a cement shop opened in the town close to the village and the new primary school was built in masonry and concrete. We fear that industrial materials and systems will replace traditionally used timber structures.

Our goal was to explore how the traditional timber system could be combined with contemporary architecture. At least for now, the traditional system is still widely used in this region and I hope we were able to promote its use by building a contemporary building. For me the critical question is "Who is coming to whose home?" and my answer is: "Homecoming is really about discovery through tracing roots." Only in that way, is one able to find one's home.

This article is an edited transcript from the Homecoming Symposium, April 13, 2012.

◄ The model is the most efficient way to communicate the building idea on site.

► Long Zhanwen is working on the beam and column connection.

▼ The finished structure of the museum uses the traditional nail-less mortise and tenon (*sun mao*) joint system.

◀ Chengdu, 2009. The idea for the form of the memorial came from the typical relief tents used in the earthquake zone. The exterior is rendered —a technique that is common in Chinese urban areas. The interior is painted with the girl's favorite color—pink—and is lined with the remaining items of her short life. Light penetrates down from a round skylight —making this tiny space pure and charming. This memorial is not only for one ordinary girl: at the 2008 Sichuan earthquake 68,712 people died and of those 5,335 were students.

Rebirth Bricks

by Liu Jiakun

The Rebirth Brick idea began with the Great Sichuan earthquake, on May 12, 2008. The earthquake created a ruin: an overwhelming amount of destruction. It was an enormous and ominous task to clear up all the debris. As it happened to be the month of May there was plentiful straw after the harvest, which farmers would use to burn for energy. I realized that the debris together with the straw could be used as an aggregate for new building materials. In some of the local manufacturing workshops, people made bricks by using just a small, mechanical device. This idea used the debris as recycled material and reactivated the productivity of the factories to create employment to manufacture these urgent materials for the reconstruction effort.

We took part in several reconstruction projects where we used the Rebirth Brick. The brick is highly relevant to the phenomenon of massive demolition happening in all cities, and goes beyond being an emergency stop-gap measure for post-earthquake rebuilding. Many forms of waste can be used as a resource for the mixture. The process of construction and demolition in a city creates infinite resources for making the bricks. A large-scale factory has been set up to recycle the debris to produce the bricks. As it costs money to get rid of the debris elsewhere, developers and construction workers have agreed to pile the debris up for us, because we will pick it up free of charge. So far the factory has collected huge mountains of debris, which can be used for many years.

We have done a lot of research and tests. We have developed a variety of Rebirth Bricks for wall construction, paving, and flooring. While the bricks with exposed aggregate can be used as external wall finishes, floor tiles can also be used as the porous base layer for large concrete surfaces.

Rebirth Bricks are becoming widely used elsewhere too. For example, an environmentally minded Swiss company welcomed the idea to build their office in Shanghai using the bricks.

Since the earthquake, I have worked mainly on reconstruction projects and it wasn't until the second half of 2010 when I finally began to work on other projects; however, the Rebirth Bricks are used in all our new projects.

During the period of post-earthquake reconstruction, I have worked on two projects without being commissioned: the first was the Rebirth Brick itself and the second was a memorial built for a little girl, Hu Huishan. Casualties in a disaster are just a statistic to the government. Every life, though, is significant. As the Chinese government has never built a memorial for common people, I wanted to build one for the little girl who died in the earthquake. It is the smallest memorial in the world—just as big as a relief tent. This link was significant, as the relief tent symbolically was part of our collective memory of the earthquake. As the memorial is politically sensitive it is not open to the public. (Many friends wanted to visit the memorial, so I have installed a peephole in the door so one can take a glimpse.)

▲ Ruin and
destruction
created by the
2008 Sichuan
earthquake.

▲ Rebirth Brick
samples showing
different forms
and debris in the
mixture.

I have done a lot of architectural design—some are personal statements expressing my own design identity. Though this memorial is a very small building project, I think it is a very important point in my career. I paid so much effort to be minimal, to be as simple and plain as possible, to let go of myself—to be selfless. A lot of people asked me "why did I not design something elaborate, something with a lot of details".

Ever since we obtained our architectural education, we have been taught to express ourselves, partially for fear that if we did not, others might think we are unable to design. But within this tiny building, and also with the idea of the Rebirth Brick, I tried very hard to dismiss this urge to design. It is actually much harder to *not design* than to design. Self-motivated projects offer one spiritual liberation and therefore are more authentic and conscientious. Sometimes these projects are a form of self-exploration.

Post-earthquake projects are projects finished under extreme conditions. This encourages designers to evaluate their role as architects and the essential aspects of architecture itself. For instance, in village reconstruction projects I recognized my role more clearly as a professional offering knowledge in order to help. In the Rebirth Brick project I focused more on analyzing costs; the higher the cost, the less convincing it appears. Finally in the creation of the memorial, emotional expression exceeded the display of personal character and style. In other words, the post-earthquake experience challenged my work to be more honest, realistic, and genuine.

This article is an edited transcript from the lecture "Right Now—Right Time," November 16, 2012 at the University of Hong Kong.

▲ By reusing the building debris as aggregate and mixing it with straw, people can make the lightweight blocks by hand during the reconstruction.

▶ Today, the process has become mechanized, creating an environmentally friendly building material with various types and commercial prices, which can be widely used in rural and urban construction.

▼ Rebirth Bricks used by villagers in Wenchuan County during the reconstruction.

◀ Chongken
Elementary
School,
Chongken, 2001.

Courtyard Typology

Or "Fog Enters the Basilica"

by Wang Weijen

Courtyard and Fog

"... I saw the fog enter the basilica, as I often love to watch it penetrate the Galleria in Milan: it is the unforeseen elements that modify and alter, like light and shadow, like stones worn smooth by the feet and hands of generations of men. Perhaps this alone was what interested me in architecture: I knew that architecture was made possible by the confrontation of a precise form with time and the elements, a confrontation which lasted until the form was destroyed in the process of this combat. Architecture was one of the ways that humanity had sought to survive; it was a way of expressing the fundamental search for happiness." [1]

Aldo Rossi, *A Scientific Autobiography*

My interest (or obsession) with the courtyard as a building typology for study and design came from my epistemological and phenomenological understanding of architecture in the early years of my education. The five-by-five meter square of blue sky and white cloud, framed by the courtyard house in a fishing village in Taiwan, was my first survey exercise; the courtyard brought light and air into the center of the house and created a microclimate with moving traces of sunlight and shadow throughout the day. These changes moderated the rhythm of the inhabitants' daily life: gardening and exercise, reading and playing, eating lunch, napping, afternoon tea, dinner, and late night conversations. This small courtyard, surrounded by eight other indoor rooms, connected a piece of framed nature with the domestic living environment. The courtyard is a particular urban artifact and a precise architecture type in the village where I lived. Looking back it is also the main source of one's humanity through natural inspiration: wind, rain, trees, birds, stars, and moonlight; just like Rossi's fog in the basilica.

I continued my study of the transformation of the courtyard house initially as an anthropologist or archeologist. I did not incorporate it as a method of design until the late 1990s. The design of the Music School in Tainan was a first attempt to organize a campus with a sequence of open courtyards arrayed across the landscape. The L-shaped dormitory was open to the hills, while the linear bars of music practice rooms stretched outwards, extending orderly into the prairie fields. Another axis of elevated pedestrian walkways cut perpendicularly through the courtyard sequence, creating large open views of the adjacent rolling hills and mountains. Although the intention of the layout to frame the landscape was horizontal in nature, the buildings are all four-story in height and the scale is much bigger than a house. The courtyards became open landscapes for young dedicated musicians walking along the corridor looking beyond the fields; between their music and landscape, sunrise and sunset, like monks in a monastery.

I began designing by asking: What is the quality of rural and urban courtyards and how do they work as individual elements? What are the systems of their fabrication and how are they patterned to make urban spaces? How do we sustain qualities of such architectural types that are challenged and must transform? How do such typologies provide the capacity to sustain continuity and at the same time facilitate new possibilities?

Courtyard as Typology

To address the issue of appropriate scale and also make the courtyard a central principle for organizing spaces, the 1999 competition for Xian Jiaotong University initiated new design methods based on the courtyard as a typology. In the following few years, a series of designs were launched, starting with the Guanglong School as a two-story model and then the Lingnan College as an eight-story model. Each explored how the traditional courtyard typology could be transformed into a spatial-form of multi-leveled courtyards, while also sustaining the experiences and characteristics of the courtyard, such as the piece of blue sky framed by a small atrium.

For Guanglong School, which has over 50 classrooms and 2,000 students, the design challenge was how to make intimately scaled spaces, creating clusters to establish better spatial identities for smaller groups. By interlocking, rotating, and overlapping single-leveled linear classroom blocks, the project created a series of interconnected courtyards of ten-by-ten meters. The upper level classrooms facing a north-south direction provided shading for the classrooms of the lower level that faced an east-west direction. Each classroom in the school was able to have its own courtyard with a large tree on the ground level, or have terraced gardens that enjoyed the treetops on the upper level. The rich spatial experiences transform the school into a village, allowing children to wander and explore, growing up inbetween large and small-scaled spaces.

The Community Collage of Lingnan University was developed three years later as the subsequent model of an eight-story prototype. Trying to preserve the existing trees and landform of the site, the design overlapped, interlocked, and offset two-storied modular blocks for teaching programs, establishing a three-dimensional system for multi-leveled courtyard spaces. It illustrates how new forms of open courtyards are shaped on the ground level, and also on the upper levels, activating programs and landscapes at each strategic datum. By studying and testing a series of sectional relationships on the site, the design created various in-between shaded courtyard spaces in the hot and humid climate of southern China. This formulated new climatic zones which facilitate natural light and ventilation. The spatial forms generate rich experiences of continuous indoor-outdoor, light-dark spatial rhythms, as well as a system of sky gardens and decks on upper levels.

With density and height increases, courtyard spaces can not only evolve from horizontal in plan to vertical in section. They also transform from private to semi-public or public spaces. The Community College of Hong Kong Polytechnic University was a breakthrough in adopting the sectional courtyard in a tower typology. While different hierarchies of layered courtyard spaces are generated for new urban conditions, critical issues of each condition are identified and reviewed: dimension, scale, movement, light, ventilation, and use.

Courtyard and Landscape

Two post-earthquake elementary schools in Taiwan, Fuming and Chongken, built in the early 2000s, were also critical moments in my design trajectory opening up exploration of architecture with the landscape. In the post-earthquake reconstruction, the remaining trees were preserved as the anchor to sustain the memory of a place, with narrative spaces developed around the trees. The notion of the courtyard as a grid-module for organizing the building was relaxed and the courtyard became a tool to set up a relationship between architecture and the landscape; a way for the building to work with nature.

In the Xixi wetland, the design developed from a twelfth-century theory on Chinese landscape painting. New spatial forms and building fabric were shaped for opening architecture to the landscape. Through the composition of a series of architectural viewing instruments each designed for different positions and viewing angles, the project intends to redefine the process of moving and viewing (*mo-vie*) and reframe our scenic experiences, exploring new conditions for our perceptions towards landscape, mountains and water.

The recent design of Choi Yuan Ecological Village is a community rehabilitation project in rural Hong Kong. The planning examines sustainable design measures including conserving fishponds and orchards, the allocation of communal land for organic farming, public spaces and infrastructures with measures for water collection and recycling.

The courtyard as typology is a strategy to bring landscape into architecture, and is similar to our desire to bring gardens or parks into the city over the last few centuries. Whether the intention is to adopt courtyard in the house or to plan a park in the city, these designs were constant negotiations between urban and rural, architecture and landscape, house and garden, manmade and nature.

Urban Courtyardism

"A city should embrace a hierarchy of superimposed configurative systems multilaterally conceived (a quantitative not a qualitative hierarchy). The finer grained systems—those which embrace the multiplied dwelling and its extension—should reflect the qualities of ascending repetitive configurative stages as has already been put forward. All systems should be familiarized one with the other in such a way that their combined impact and interaction can be appreciated as a single complex system—polyphonal, multirhythmic, kaleidoscopic and yet perpetually and everywhere comprehensible. A single homogeneous configuration composed of many subsystems, each covering the same overall area and equally valid, but each with a different grain, scale of movement and association-potential. These systems are to be so configured that one evolved out from the other—is part of it. The specific meaning of each system must sustain the meaning of the other."

Francis Strauven, *Aldo Van Eyck: The Shape of Relativity.* [2]

These works demonstrate how to reinvent the historical courtyard typology for contemporary urban conditions and also illustrate the possibilities of establishing a new spatial form as an urban fabric, one that is able to generate permeable urban experiences of indoor-outdoor, semi-public and private spatial rhythms in contemporary urban conditions. It is the exploration of appropriate scales and heights for courtyard dimensions under different situations: climate, lighting, ventilation, view, utility, and access. It also provides a platform of imagination towards an "urban courtyardism" for our cities and architecture, one that is capable of facing challenges of density, porosity, public spaces, and sustainability.

It is also about the fog entering the basilica: *"It is the unforeseen elements that modify and alter, like light and shadow, like stones worn smooth by the feet and hands of generations of men."* [3]

(1)   Rossi, Aldo. 1984. *A scientific autobiography*. Cambridge (US) 1984.
(2)   Francis Strauven. *Aldo Van Eyck: The Shape of Relativity*. Amsterdam, 1998.
(3)   Rossi, Aldo. 1984. ibid.

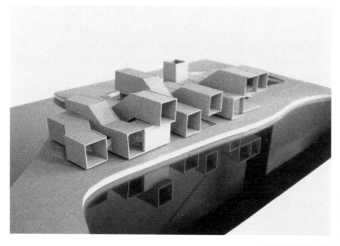

◀ Landscape as courtyard: Xixi Wetland Art Village, Hangzhou, Zhejiang, 2011.

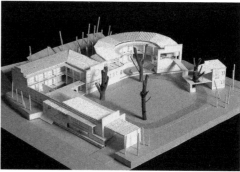

▼ Village houses and courtyard: New Choi Yuen Village Eco-House Design, Hong Kong, 2011.

▶ Courtyard as landscape: Chongken Elementary School, Chongken, 2001.

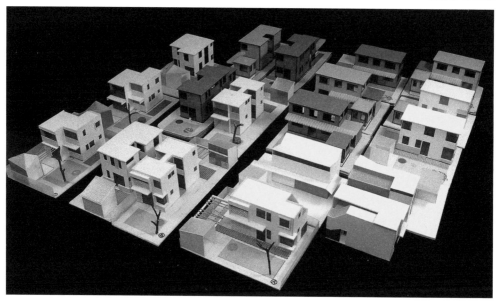

▲ Multilevel
courtyard:
Community
College, Lingnan
University, Hong
Kong, 2011.

◀ Sectional
courtyard: Hong
Kong Polytechnic
University,
Community
College, Hong
Kong, 2009.

◄ One of the main
intentions of the
Shijia Village
House is to resist
the villagers'
increasing
dependency on
outside goods and
services. For now
the house will
be both a home
for women in need
as well as a new
center of women's
handicraft.
It becomes both
domestic and
communal,
a bridge between
the individual
and collective
spirit of a village.

A House for All Seasons

Making Architecture in a Place without Architecture

by John Lin

In Fall 2006 I first visited Shijia Village in Shaanxi Province with the Shaanxi Women's Federation and the Luke Him Sau Charitable Trust. Initially, the villagers provided us with a list of requests. The villagers hoped to build an expensive infrastructure network to pipe water down from the mountains and avoid having to pay government taxes for their existing water supply. However, we wanted to find a way to make a project that actually empowered them to solve problems on their own. After some investigation it was decided to help build one prototype house. This house would be a model, or reference, which contained ideas for sustainable living. It included a solution for rainwater collection from the roof and helped to allow the villagers to be more self-reliant. The design incorporated traditional materials such as mud bricks with a cast concrete structure. The intention from the start was not to duplicate a single house design throughout the village. (The villagers are currently involved in an ongoing process of renovating their houses.) Instead we wanted to preserve the diversity of individual solutions and simply inform that process by demonstrating ways of combining traditional and contemporary ideas.

The following summer a group of students from the University of Hong Kong went to Shijia Village. The students conducted research and documented each of the village houses. The intention was to assemble a brief for the house design and to understand the dramatic changes in villagers' lifestyle and livelihood. We wanted to begin from the ground up and not take *anything* for granted. The notion of a traditional village no longer exists. The process of urbanization over the past 30 years has created a reliance on the city as a primary source of income. As a result the city has also become the model for development. It was important to record and understand the complexities of the village during this change.

All houses in Shijia Village and the surrounding region are originally of mud brick construction and occupy parcels of the same configuration: 10 × 30 m. The houses are each in the midst of a long process of change as villagers gradually renovate and build upon the courtyard typology. Often the courtyard itself is eliminated, or three-story concrete structures are built while 100-year-old houses are turned into animal and storage sheds. Apart from the identically defined parcel boundary, no two houses are alike. The students documented and interviewed various families in the village, collectively compiling a portrait of the modern Chinese village house: a portrait not only of building types but of a lifestyle in transition.

In China, rural livelihood is perhaps best expressed through the utilization of the domestic courtyard, where much of life takes place. Indeed, the majority of a village's open space is contained within the walls of the house. This sets up an intimate relationship between the courtyard and other interior rooms that is both visual and functional. The prototype house design includes four functional courtyards as the primary elements of the house. The courtyards are inserted throughout the house to relate to the main rooms: kitchen, bathroom, living room, bedrooms. In addition each courtyard is spatially unique and one could say the house is designed around the courtyards.

The title "House For All Seasons" is a statement on how the design redefined the program of a rural house. It is a reaction against the prevalence of generic multi-story concrete, brick, and tiled village houses. These constructions are taking place in every village in China. They look the same whether they are located far to the north or south. Generic buildings are replacing very specific vernacular house types, which have adapted gradually over hundreds of years to the climate and location where they exist.

To this day the program continues to evolve. For now the house will be both a home for women in need, as well as a new center of women's handicraft. It becomes both domestic and communal, a bridge between the individual and collective identity of the village. The construction of the house has begun a new phase in which a cooperative business, around traditional straw weaving, is being developed. The local Women's Federation and the donor continue to work together to empower village women through the marketing of their own traditional crafts in a modern world. Even the furniture in the house is an adaptation of traditional techniques for modern use. Rather than accepting the influence of cities and accepting the necessity of consumer products, the house project reasserts the independent spirit of the village.

The reality of working in rural areas is that the profession of architecture does not exist in villages. So, what can an architect do in a place with no need for architecture? In cities throughout China architects are in great demand; however this means the fees are low and the work is driven by speed and efficiency. This leaves little room for speculation and exploration of a larger social agenda. On the contrary, doing architecture in villages is a unique opportunity to rethink the role of the architect since it begins without such a clear necessity. As a non-profit research and design organization, we offer our services to charities and governments. We don't work with or for a single client but with a community of people. Often we work to create projects from scratch, simply by examining the conditions which are present and addressing the problems we see. Afterwards we find the means to fund and build the project. Naturally, the project evolves over time. This is the most significant contribution of our work. It goes beyond good design. It examines the question of basic necessity. It involves the creation of new programs and projects in order to find alternative approaches to rural development. This also reflects an alternative way of working as an architect.

◀ Traditional houses in Shijia Village are originally of mud brick construction and occupy parcels of the same configuration: 10 × 30 meters. The process of rural development increasingly favors the destruction and abandonment of the traditional in favor of the new.

◀ Newly built house in Shijia Village with patterned tiling. As the houses transform from the traditional mud brick to concrete and tile, the construction process itself has been radically altered.

▼ The Shijia Village House prototype attempts to preserve the intelligence of local materials and techniques. A concrete column and roof structure is combined with mud brick infill walls mud brick being a traditional means of insulation.

▲ Building of the underground biogas system. The courtyards house pigs, and an underground biogas system produces energy for cooking.

▲ Building of the mud brick wall.

▼ Piles of bricks for the Shijia Village House.

▲ The entire outside wall of the house is wrapped in a brick screen. This not only serves to protect the mud walls, but also shades windows and openings.

▲ Village contractor.

◀ Builders live on site during the construction.

◀ Source of
inspiration for the
Village Mountains:
the Lotus and
Dragon Head
mountain in
Guilin during
the Yangshuo
Storefront project
in 2005.

Village Mountains

Urban Agricultural Infrastructure

Zhang Ke in Conversation with Cruz Garcia

From 2010 to 2015 the hunger for urbanization in China has devoured 12 million acres of land per year and a staggering 150 million acres of arable land were consumed by urban sprawl from 1996 to 2010. Facing these revealing figures and concerned about the struggle of the growing urban area versus the decreasing arable area, standardarchitecture has proposed a solution in the form of a colossal infrastructural hybrid that integrates architecture and urbanism, the countryside and the city.

The Village Mountains proposal offers a vision for a new form of urbanism in which arable land and the urban, infrastructure and architecture become one. Cruz Garcia (WAI Think Tank) discusses with standardarchitecture's founding principal Zhang Ke the concepts and theories that drive the Village Mountains proposal and the evolution of his vision for the future of the city.

Cruz Garcia: Could you start by telling us how your interest in the relationship between agriculture, architecture, and the city became manifest in some of your projects? As we have noticed, the Village Mountains seem to be a continuation of a developing concept that dates back to the art project of Un-natural Growth (Formica Art Exhibition) to the project presented at the Hong Kong-Shenzhen Biennale (2007–08) and eventually to the projects you have presented at the Chengdu Biennale (2011) and at the design weeks in Milan and Beijing.

Zhang Ke: At the Hong Kong-Shenzhen Biennale the question of what the rural should

be, or could be in the future, was not yet being addressed. Back then, with the West Kowloon Mountains, we were interested in how agriculture could be brought into an urban area, and how agriculture could be a strategy for urbanism.

However, before the Biennale we were already working on mixing mountains and agriculture with urbanism during our Yangshuo Storefront project; we built a small storefront among the mountains. I think this was the first time that we were inspired to discover how someone can live around, among, and inside the mountains and how we could merge these findings with our urban imagination. It was the *most* Chinese landscape that was the inspiration, the first step—that's how the inspiration came to us.

Cruz Garcia: Although this was the first step, it didn't have form yet. How did the concept evolve from the Yangshuo project to the Un-natural Growth project and the work exhibited in the biennales and design weeks? How did the idea evolve from the inspiring experience of building in such a powerful landscape to the Village Mountains?

Zhang Ke: I would like to elaborate a little bit more about the West Kowloon Mountains project. Of course at that time, in 2007, nobody really talked about agriculture. It was still the peak of a frenzied time. But then when everybody was so infatuated about *this crazy thing*, it became a matter of gaining even more attention—to make people think and ask: "Does our urbanism have to be in opposition to agriculture? Can they coexist in the same space at the same time?"

Agriculture usually and naturally occupies the outer surfaces of the settled space and urban life occupies most of the inside. And then, of course, there's an overlap. So if you bring agriculture back into the city, in a massive way, as we did when we designed terraced slants with rice fields, which we called Rice Field Skyscrapers, it can bring a completely new urban experience, an almost rural experience which is desperately craved by urban dwellers. Although it was the time of the financial peak, 2007 was also the beginning of the global food shortage. The project became a provocation: we wanted to throw a stone into the water and see the ripple effect. The project was less about a solution, and more about and exploring an idea and making a statement.

Cruz Garcia: The Rice Field Skyscrapers were a statement, not a project? Was that the beginning of your interest in urban infrastructures for agriculture?

Zhang Ke: Not only, it was also a critique of what I thought was wrong with the West Kowloon land reclamation and planning at that time. Of course, Hong Kong is the world's most urbanized place, but why do you build this huge artificial landfill, which took a huge amount of public money? Originally Norman Foster proposed to cover the site with a big shell, which seemed ridiculous in a hot tropical environment, which then led to the idea of a series of buildings—some cultural projects here and there—which seemed like a strategy that was not financially sustainable at all.

So what we were proposing was actually smart. With the budget of a huge landfill we created a mixture with a balanced program.

On the one hand we proposed the world's tallest department store for the inside of the skyscraper—which basically is what defines Hong Kong—embedding (like jewels in the mountain) cultural facilities, galleries, and theaters while on the outside of the building, we offered an agricultural urban experience that can be explored by all the citizens of the city—which is what Hong Kong is lacking.

This was the first time we started tackling the relationship between a futuristic human-made infrastructure and an urban infrastructure, in correlation with agriculture.

Cruz Garcia: The Rice Field Skyscrapers raise the provocation: "If you're going to make all this effort to make something absurd, at least make it sustainable?"

Zhang Ke: The funny thing is although most people think it's absurd, it is actually the most needed. So for me it's the least absurd. I don't even think it looked absurd. It's just that nobody really thought of it before. Look at the mountains through the eyes of a child. Children love the idea of the Rice Field Skyscrapers because they don't think it's absurd, they think, "Wow great! We can play on the outside surface of the building!"

Cruz Garcia: In your Beijing Plan for 2030, the Village Mountains were set into the periphery of Beijing as a new efficient linear center, with a highly efficient mass transport system to free the city center from cars and to leave space for agriculture. This project was based on numbers, discovered during your research. Did the subsequent projects also respond to statistics?

Zhang Ke: When I did the research for the Chengdu Biennale in 2011 I discovered that in China, as everywhere else, urban expansion invades agricultural land. Then, if you want

to expand agricultural production, you're not only increasing the per-acre production, you need to expand your arable area by decreasing the urban areas. So we asked if there is a way that urban expansion and agricultural expansion could work together. The conflict between urban expansion and decreasing arable area is becoming critical as our population grows: we have already reached seven billion. Today, there's a lack of food. From 1996 to 2010, within only 15 years, we lost 8% of the overall arable area—we lost 150 million acres. Altogether we have only 950 million acres left!

Cruz Garcia: But why does the population keep growing while at the same time, a particular problem starts to show in China, that land is turning arid and desertification is occurring?

Zhang Ke: In China's urbanization, the expansion of the settlements grow out rather than up—it sprawls, so that the area of the urban expansion eats up too much arable area, and this is threatening the food safety of China. As designers, we are not only looking at small-scale design, we also look at the large-scale, the overall picture of what's happening in the world. It is not absurd to think that in 30 years there will be starvation in China, if we don't do something, if we just keep up the current urbanization rates, without any vision.

Cruz Garcia: Do you think these issues can be solved through architecture? Or does it imply that there needs to be more policies to control urbanization? What if we forbid developers to take over any of the arable lands? In other places these problems are handled by other means. Given that designers have limited influence and power, we would need responsible clients, we would need somebody to listen.

Zhang Ke: This is exactly the opposite of what I am thinking. As architects and planners in China we can't just wait for clients to come to us. If we don't think actively about issues and keep proposing solutions, I don't think people are able to foresee and imagine the incredibly dangerous situation we are facing in future. This is not a scary invented situation—it is real. I really think that architects and designers, or at least a small group of them, need to consider the overall picture. They need to figure out what's wrong with the current situation and then they need to really go out to state: "Hey look here, there is a problem!" Of course the Village Mountains are a call for attention, stating that for rural development and urban development we simply don't have enough surface and so we need to go vertical.

But we don't want to go vertical in the traditional way. What if we can go vertical in a way that becomes a more desirable way of living? What if it is a way in which people can still be provided with a diverse dream of living in which arable and urban spaces are mixed, with each person having their own cubic meter of space where they can decide how they want to build their houses, their lives? They can have little chicken coops or pig yards in front or at the back of their houses...

Cruz Garcia: I understand that the Rice Field Skyscrapers for Kowloon were more of a statement, is the Village Mountains proposal also a statement?

Zhang Ke: I think so far it's a call for attention. It is still a statement. It's even more eye-catching, but at the same time I believe that it can be real. Or it will be real, maybe in one decade? It's structurally, mechanically, and financially doable. It's a new way of development and it shows that land and real estate development can be more vertical and at the same time rural. If you think rural is horizontal, or urban is vertical, then my question is: can we be vertical and rural? The Village Mountains really trigger the imagination for a new way of living which, in the most unexpected way, links to the ancient Chinese intellectual dream of living: If you have a *vita contemplativa* in the mountains, you hide yourself in the mountains, with a view of your life staring back into the city.

In the Village Mountains you can live in the mountain, albeit in an artificial mountain. But this artificial mountain might be even more beautiful and more dwellable than a real mountain. At the same time it could be the most sustainable way for you to move around, because you simply go up and down; whenever you go down you have a subway or light rail so you don't need to drive cars.

Cruz Garcia: So it becomes urban?

Zhang Ke: It's an urban-rural environment. It's a way to maintain the rural environment in an urban life setting. It's a new way of development because you don't need to live in a big, stiff building; it is vertical infrastructure for people. In that way all people can buy metric meters of space and build their own houses.

Cruz Garcia: Is the proposal related to the 1960s and the need for reconstruction and multiprogram solutions after the Second World War? Everybody at this time was imagining infrastructures for urban development: from the Metabolists to the post-war avant-garde in Europe. Most of these proposed urban infrastructures were idealistic. Do you want the Village Mountains to be read in this utopian context? You're affirming that this can be done, at least in China.

Zhang Ke: It is both futuristic and realistic, and I guess also an ancient desire. And of course it's sustainable because it saves

farmland and produces farmland. You can even grow food on your own, in your front yard. I think it's a new kind of "utopia," which can be realized. It then becomes fundamental to rethink the relationship between the rural and the urban. Can the rural be urban? Can the urban be rural? That might be the real direction of the future.

Cruz Garcia: Does that create another polemic for our profession and what architects do in this society? Maybe we don't need them anymore?

Zhang Ke: No, we need them to be more active. I think we need to invent a new profession, which is actively thinking of the surface of the earth. We need to be thinking about how to manage the surface of the earth and, at the same time, executing the vision of replanning and redesigning this surface. With the earth's population being doubled and tripled, you're not talking anymore about clusters of a human-occupied surface. Pretty soon all inhabitable surface, except for desert and water, is going to be occupied. Then, how do you manage it? Is there a way to control it? Is there a way that we still can grow? Can the earth's surface sustain the growth of the population?

I believe it's possible as long as you manage it well. And I believe that the living quality can be even better. We can make our cities consume less energy and also be productive. This might be a naïve thought, but I think it's fun to imagine.

▲ The Village
Mountains
propose a universal
strategy for the
co-existence of
city and farmland.
With curtilage
properties
allocated to
each household,
residents are
able to construct
their homes inside
the nests and
keep poultry
around the house.

▲ The Village
Mountains at the
Milano Design
Week, April 2012.

C

Practicing the Rural

In China, the rural is a key agent in the process of urbanization. The unique differences between rural and urban land, rural citizens and urban citizens, have led to specific forms of development. Despite the resultant conversion of rural land into built form, architects have been predominantly absent from this process. By choosing to work in rural areas, or through responding to China's unique urban-rural tension, the architects in Practicing the Rural are developing discursive ideas and provocative buildings. For these architects the rural is a rich source for experimentation and a clear counterpoint to other modes of architectural production in China. Through engaging in the distinct characteristics of a local, rural context, can these alternative forms of practice generate and advance contemporary architecture in China?

Expanding the Field

Position by Joshua Bolchover

Ever since China's economic reformation, the emergence of instant cities and iconic skylines has been coupled with vast swaths of urbanized matter in the form of factories, migrant housing, residential towers, and a hinterland of semi-industrialized and semi-agricultural landscapes. These sites of indeterminate fabric are often legally designated as rural, despite being highly urbanized. In this respect the countryside in China is multifaceted. On one level it can materialize as a seething mess of generic buildings, incomplete construction, and fragmented territories and on the other it can still appear bucolic, with traditional village houses and rice terraces. However, within these rural conditions, the construction of anomalous tiled, concrete houses reflects the remittances being sent back from family members working within urbanized regions. The rural is not simply an agrarian support structure for cities. Paradoxically, although the urban and rural have remained intertwined, their citizens have grown further apart due to the ever-widening economic polarization between the urban rich and the rural poor.

If this describes a physical context in transition, then how has the context of architectural practice also adapted to these transformations since 1978? The majority of architectural practice in China is still predominantly the remit of large, state-owned design institutes, conglomerates of engineers and architects that conduct all the service requirements necessary for construction. Large institutes such as the Beijing Institute of Architectural Design have nearly 2,000 employees and have conducted over 3,700 projects within the last 10 years alone. There are other organizations known as government-owned but commercially operated entities, but these follow a similar model compared with the prevalent Western concept of privately owned, individually authored signature offices. However this is changing: since 1993 the Ministry of Construction began experimenting with private architectural practice, allowing some to start up, and as late as the year 2000 the operation of private firms was sanctioned at a national scale. In parallel, architectural education has also undergone a period of "opening up" with many Western architecture schools collaborating with prestigious PRC schools and many Chinese graduates attending masters programs in the United States or Europe.

The objective of discussing what "practicing the rural" means in China is two-fold. Firstly it raises the issue of what constitutes the practice of being an architect and secondly it addresses how one, as an architect, can respond to the specific issues engendered by this rural context in flux. Each of the architects represented in this section take a unique stance with respect to the role of the architect or through developing unique methodologies.

Tong Ming considers the countryside to be an artificial construct, constantly manipulated and managed by human intervention. He uses the example of the *Wei*, an agrarian morphology that can mediate between natural processes and human settlement, offering the potential to create coexistence and synergies between the urban and rural. He calls for furthering the discourse to disassemble these constructs through finding clues in these ancient artifacts.

Huang ShengYuan openly fell in love with the Taiwanese countryside 17 years ago and his contribution is an ode to the virtues of the pastoral: an idyll that reflects his choice as an architect to adopt an alternative lifestyle whereby work and pleasure are interchangeable. Rather than adopt the mode of the global, jet-set architect, Huang has committed himself to work in one location, working for, and as part of a community with a vested interest in its future.

Hsieh Ying-chun is a self-described architect and contractor. Through using a kit-of-parts structure that can be easily assembled, he creates a support infrastructure for others to complete however they choose. Each project becomes a participatory process allowing the community to play a role in shaping their own environment. This DIY engagement advocates a lack of design control for the architect, dispelling the idea of the architect as signature style-maker.

Drawing on two sources of inspiration, the *tulou* earth buildings in Fujian and urban villages that exist throughout urbanized areas of China, the work of Urbanus Research Bureau attempts to transfer these typologies, adapting them to new settings. The archetype of the *tulou* as a condensed urban model within a rural context is deployed in an urban context for migrant (rural) workers. The urban village represents a collective, social form of living evidencing forms of urban life that are not present within the formal city that encapsulates them. The interplay between rural and urban typologies registers the role of the rural in China's urbanization process, and activates the role of ruralism as a methodology to address prescient urban issues such as economic polarization or divisions in citizen status.

These architects are not vernacular architects and they cannot be grouped under a shared ideological framework or architectural approach. Their methodologies are not necessarily the most original or unique when considering other practices from around the world. Their specificity and pioneering nature is through their engagement with two contexts undergoing radical transformation: the rural and architectural practice in China. Each requires urgent redefinition. Through their situatedness and commitment to experimentation, these architects have created the foundation for an expanded field of practice.

◀ *Wei* unit in the
Tai-lake region.

The Wei

Rural Lesson for Contemporary Urban Architects

by Tong Ming

There is a Chinese saying "Where there is a building there is a city." People usually think architecture is the sociocultural product of human beings. We think buildings in the city embody the story of our civilization, but the wild countryside doesn't have any of this. However, the countryside is not as wild as we think it is, in reality it is 100% an artifact. The organization of the *Wei* in the Tai-lake region in the eastern part of China originated 2,000 years ago and continued to evolve alongside the development of the human settlement in the area.

The *Wei* is an embankment that encloses a patch of land to create a flood-free plot so that it can be cultivated. Irrigation water is channeled from the surrounding rivers and controlled by sluice gates. Every altitude level in the *Wei* has a function and the differences in elevation are used to adjust the direction of water flow in order to ensure that every plot of farmland can be irrigated or drained if necessary. The original settlers used canals and ditches to define and form this fertile and productive area. The *Wei* covered almost the entire region of the Yangtze Delta. Even a small part of one *Wei* unit demonstrates that the farmland and houses are very carefully and elegantly organized to create a very efficient relationship between working and living.

Originally every *Wei* was an independent unit, able to continuously adjust its size according to political, economic, or social development. At the same time, the *Wei* regulated its productiveness according to the water supply and the condition of natural resources. For a long time, the comprehensive coordination of the *Wei* fabric ensured and sustained life in this part of rural China. The *Wei* unit can also be understood as a community unit. People shared a collective will and interest to live together in the *Wei* for reasons of security, social life, trade, and provision of food. For a long time villagers of one *Wei* belonged to the same big family.

The *Wei* organization produced a unique pattern in the rural landscape in the Tai-lake region. This gridded system later became the infrastructure for future human habitation: first villages and later cities originated from the *Wei*. Two different typologies evolved that are typical of the region: the water towns and the canal cities. Modifications of the *Wei* usually resulted in alteration of these communities. Although the *Wei* underwent a big adjustment process in the 1950s to pursue large-scale farming, the main figuration of the *Wei* system still remains.

However, ongoing rural construction and the development of the Tai-lake region caused by the relocation of people have initiated large modifications to the farmland. This has caused drastic change to the social structure and local culture. The historic and unique rural ecology of the *Wei* is about to disappear. People replace it with imported agricultural and urban landscapes that are supposedly more scientific or advanced in ways of production. But in fact, compared with the *Wei* structure, they are neither more social nor ecological.

In the past 30 years, the soaring economy of China has triggered high-speed development. During this process, the rapid transformation of Chinese cities is well known, but the destruction of the countryside has not yet received much attention. Rural fabric has been erased and the relationship between the rural and the urban has been inverted, changing people's lifestyles as well as their methods of communication. Moreover, the ideology of the relationship between humans and nature is about to collapse. The cities and the countryside around the Tai-lake region are under threat in terms of their culture and history. How to preserve and retain the intelligence from our traditions is the challenge for contemporary Chinese architecture both in the city and the countryside. Reading and understanding the *Wei* can help us better understand our cities, our countryside, and most importantly their coexistence.

Therefore, as Chinese architects, we need to go back and learn from the traditional rural system and be introspective when considering how to modernize the countryside. Through this approach we can create a harmonious relationship between human activity and nature and develop an intelligence of construction that can coexist with the landscape. We not only decipher and reinterpret the differing relationships that we have with the world, but also reassess the values of traditional architecture versus modern techniques.

Further research is necessary to develop an architectural language that reconnects with tradition and at the same time is based on the reality of contemporary construction. If we can promote a kind of architectural activity that can go beyond the barriers between urban and rural, and if we can try to absorb the intelligence that resides in ancient artifacts like the *Wei*, we will be able to establish a productive dialogue between architecture and its surroundings. That way, we may be able to cope with this era of revolution.

▲ *Wei* organization, being invaded by modern industrial development, Wujiang, Suzhou.

▶ The town and country were developed within the *Wei* organization, Tang Yue, South Anhui Province.

139

◀ Yilan is what Yilan is. The township doesn't necessarily have to follow the footsteps of the city. It is more than nostalgia. Yilan is the assembly of home that goes beyond blood ties and beyond geography, that lies somewhere within the heart.

Rural Architecture Practice

Letter to an Old Friend

by Huang ShengYuan

Dear Teacher,

Four days of clammy weather during the 228 Memorial Day holidays. The atmosphere in Fieldoffice is just like the atmosphere of other weekends: calm and quiet. Colleagues drift in and out—getting on with their everyday lives. Instead of rushing back to the city these young architects hang around with their friends in Yilan. Projects they and their seniors have done in Yilan have become special homesteads and attractors for urban people to visit. They enjoy the calm country life. I was surprised when I first heard the exchange students in the office, who are from India, Xiamen, Singapore, and Hunan saying, "Coming to Yilan is like coming back home." Later, I started to understand that through relaxing and sharing, endurance and tolerance, the spiritual concept of home exists universally.

If you ride a bike or motorcycle across the mountain, the Taipei-Yilan Boundary Park is a good place to glance at our home Yilan. There, with 20,000 metal and timber pieces and 40,000 nails, one of our projects, the Jin Mien Deck, was completed by Dun-Nan Tsai, a student recommended by you 10 years ago. He finished the project on his own with ease.

Close to the Jin Mien Deck, another project, the Cherry Orchard Cemetery, is located on the ridge of the mountain. It took five years to finish the project and Xiaohei went up the mountain to inspect the site everyday. The passageways that stow the cremation boxes stretch alongside the view of the shore. In this solemn and respectful atmosphere, family members can cherish the memory of the deceased. Viewing the Pacific Ocean, everyone is given the opportunity to gaze afar—up to the stars or down towards their homeland.

Next time you come to Yilan, you may live in the Paddy Commune. It was set up by Ye Zhao-Xian and carried on by A-Chao and Dong-Nan, and now Wen-Rui is taking good care of it. Some companions live there: the happy guys, A-Kuan and Yo-Zhong, who play guitar all the time; A-Yao who has been here since high school, and some other young guys, you may not know yet. Every day they walk along the irrigation canals to the office. It is only a five-minute walk around the bamboo fence to our innovative creative factory, our Fieldoffice.

A-Xiao, Sheng Chuan, Mary Chen, Shaokai, Taiya, Jerry Su, Min Shu, and Yen Tin are struggling with the Yilan Moat Reconstruction, which will be hopefully be finished by the end of this year. This project is part of the Yilan Revitalization Plan, a network of projects within Yilan including the Diu Diu Dang project, the future Children's Stadium, the Crescent Alley, the moat remediation on Jhongshan Park, the renovation of the

◀▼ Instead of rushing back to the city these young architects hang around with their friends in Yilan. Projects they and their seniors have done in Yilan have become special homesteads and attractors for urban people to visit. They enjoy the calm country life.

historical walkway between Dongyue Temple and Wugu Temple, the soon-to-be completed Yilan Museum of Art, the renovation of the historic city wall area, and the revitalization of the irrigation systems. The young colleagues are not afraid to encounter their first on-site supervision jobs. They are eager to learn and to gain more experience, so they ask for advice from the workers frequently.

Over the years and by interacting with local communities for the reopening of the Yilan Distillery or through encouraging people to participate in the Jin-mei Footbridge, we discovered that we Yilan people can always learn from each other. It is touching to see that everyone is trying their best to find ways to coexist with their surroundings.

Tutors and students from the school nearby tried hard to persuade the older generation to accept an energy-saving sustainable lighting concept. They asked us for a low-lighting system, so that the artificial light is not destructive. The neighbors enjoy having the new narrow footbridge attached to the existing town bridge, so that no one will stay and block the bridge anymore. Through this new path people can still bump into each other and chat. The footbridge is attached to the side of the old bridge. It is a light structure. It not only reduces the amount of construction material but also reduces the water pressure on the structure when the floods come, as water passes simply through. We invented this new structure with the Yilan River Department.

Spending time with the residents helps us to understand their real needs. Their feedback concerns public interest and reflects their spiritual idea of balance as well as compromise, which are much more precious than general answers such as "efficiency" or "the bigger the better" that you receive from

random street interviews. I learned that the environment should never be solely created around its current needs alone.

Have you noticed the small boats sitting in the office yard? They are made by colleagues and interns, under the leadership of Mr. Tseng from the Community College. Wei-Jie Wang brought him in. Staff and interns from different countries did a trial run with the boats in the small canals nearby—ending the curse for us Taiwanese being afraid of the water. Water is the essence of Yilan.

The new generation of government officials has decided against building a science and technology park by the sea. Instead, they want to preserve the fields by the shore and maintain the sanddunes. This generation who grew up in the information age realizes that long-term dedication is necessary. They treat the site they are working on as if it were their own hometown (political resistance won't stand in their way). And the actual financial profit is merely trivial to them.

After 14 years of preparation the Luo-dong Culture Center is almost complete. The cultural marketplace remains under construction and we are still fundraising. The details are carefully designed and the construction quality should be guaranteed. From the beginning, I wanted to hang up the gallery and bury the cultural marketplace underground to leave the central area empty. This creates an open and fluid public space and reveals both the mountainscape and the broad-minded attitude of Yilan people.

Thanks to Jau-Shian Yen, who was 32 years old back then, he initiated the concept of dividing the construction process into smaller stages. It is a bold concept and works like a relay between groups of young people, including Danny, who came all the way back from America on several occasions to help finalize the project. I am also thankful to the passionate young government officials and to the public who helped our office survive the process of drawing, budget estimation, construction, and political battle.

We appreciate the good governance we have these days and we are lucky to witness a Taiwan that could not have been possible in the past. This creates opportunities for cultural life to develop and opportunities for everyone to get involved. It includes dedication not out of self-interest but out of the interest for the community and the public realm. Every place can link back to its own history as well as create new legends. Growth is not about being competitive; it is not about figures, grades, or the individual.

Another student of yours, Tu, who has now become the CEO of the office, is my most respected student. Tu is always smiling and encouraging when others face difficulties. He also encourages colleagues to take exercise, do yoga, or practice English or Spanish with him and even to take courses at the Community College. Tu, Yang, and the office accountant, Shu-Chuan, always remind me to take care of colleagues. Everyone needs a home that accepts alternative minds. Being together is not about unifying, but is about looking after one another and allowing for individual space at the same time. Jason has just returned from his trip to India. A couple of years ago I asked him and Tu if they wanted to work outside Taiwan. He replied quietly that there are still many places in Taiwan that need to be taken care of.

Yilan is what Yilan is. The township doesn't necessarily have to follow the footsteps of the city. It is more than nostalgia. Yilan is the assembly of home that goes beyond blood ties and beyond geography, that lies somewhere within the heart. Since people started texting each other with cell phones, it's been quite a while since I wrote such a long letter. Seeing this, you may envy me for such a wonderful life and warm family that I'm having here.

Huang ShengYuan, 2012 spring, Fieldoffice, Yilan, Taiwan.

◄ Have you noticed the small boats sitting in the office yard? They are made by colleagues and interns, under the leadership of Mr. Tseng from the Community College. Wei-Jie Wang brought him in. Staff and interns from different countries did a trial run with the boats in the small canals nearby—ending the curse for us Taiwanese being afraid of the water.

◄▼ Over the years and by interacting with local communities for the reopening of the Yilan Distillery or through encouraging people to participate in the Jin-mei Footbridge, we discovered that we Yilan people can always learn from each other.

▲ A couple of years ago I asked him and Tu if they wanted to work outside Taiwan. He replied quietly that there are still many places in Taiwan that need to be taken care of.

◄ This woman
of Yangliu Village
is rebuilding her
house, with help of
a lightweight steel
structural frame,
after it got
destroyed during
the 2008 Sichuan
earthquake.

Sustainable Construction

Empowerment of the Villager

by Hsieh Ying-chun

Today I would like to share my experiences working in rural areas in China and how I, as an architect, got involved with building in these areas and also how I developed a working methodology that directly involves rural residents.

First let's talk about the power of rural residents. After the Great Sichuan Earthquake, on May 12, 2008, villagers built two million houses in just two years, exceeding the total amount of housing units in New York City alone! Most of these houses were built in the traditional way with very simple tools.

During the three decades following China's opening up, the amount of houses built in rural areas was four to five times higher than in the cities. It seems that no one has realized how great this number is. This massive scale of reconstruction demonstrates how powerful people are. Unfortunately, the houses that were built after China's opening up were not at all safe. These newly built houses were completely destroyed by the Sichuan earthquake, whereas in the same region traditional houses survived in good condition. Villagers spent all their lifesavings, ending up in heavy debt, just to construct these newly built homes. In other words, the most remarkable achievement in rural China after the opening up was to build crappy houses! This is without doubt caused by the current mode of housing development and is possible to avoid. It's the same situation in Haiti and maybe across the developing world. However, contemporary architectural practice entered this field yet.

In Xichuan, Henan Province, a great amount of relics belonging to the State of Chu (1042–223 BC) were excavated. The bronze-ware, with more than 2,000 years of history, was then made into a new symbol for the Cangfang town. This 2,000-year-old statue, within the newly built town center, shows the profound difference between an underlying culture and overlaying culture in China today. This is what rural China is like.

Surprisingly, most of the original village housing was built in the 1980s, only 30 years ago, which means that the same generation built both types of village houses—the original village houses as well as the crappy houses. And I would argue that the original village houses are the ones which have integrity with their environment. It seems that the connection to 2,000 years of continued building culture has been lost. Why do things happen this way?

In fact, this enormous change did not take place until recent years when the government began to build New Socialist Villages in rural China. This was the turning point and more than that, it was the unfortunate result of professionals getting involved.

With the requirement to maintain 1.8 billion acres of basic farmland, while increasing the rate of urbanization, the government has simultaneously centralized farmland and replaced whole village communities. Meanwhile the rural population continues to migrate to the cities and yet construction in rural China proceeds.

◀ Rural China built by the government: in the process of centralizing farmland the government or investors replace whole village communities with so-called New Socialist Villages.

▼ Rural China built by the villagers: In Xichuan, Henan Province, a great amount of relics belonging to the State of Chu (1042–223 BC) were excavated. The bronzeware, with more than 2,000 years of history, was then made into a new symbol for the town of Cangfang.

▼ ▶ Yangliu Village reconstruction: original village houses use stone and wood from the mountains, a material tradition which the villagers were able to maintain with help of the lightweight steel structural frame.

◀ Village opening of the Yangliu Village.

The result is a housing footprint that is becoming very inefficient in rural China. Therefore rural development has to be understood as part of the index of China's urbanization, and rural development policies have to be redesigned.

The New Socialist Village is the housing the government and investors provide for the villagers when their village is relocated. It is an image of Western suburbia placed in the rural areas of China. If this is supposed to be an indicator of our civilization, it is unacceptable!

You may think, being so wise and capable of building those traditional Chinese village houses for over 2,000 years, that the villagers should be able to solve their housing problem by themselves. But in my experience all the new materials, values, and techniques make it difficult for villagers to find their own way. The important question is: Why can't we as architects enter this field? Let's understand this problem through the idea of intersubjectivity.

Architects put too much emphasis on their own self-worth, so they cannot work with others. They can build shiny skyscrapers, but not simple village houses. I believe if you want to build the latter one, you have to give up some of your own self-worth and instead cooperate with the villagers. The question is: how can architects provide a basic organization and at the same time how can they enable communication and encourage the participation of the villagers? Since most of our methods, ideas, and technologies are new to the villagers we need to simplify the construction process. In our methodology we use (a) an open system and (b) a simplified construction process. A lightweight steel structure forms the house frame. Villagers then fill in the walls with different materials. The lightweight steel structure is very easy to use. As long as you know how to tighten a bolt,

you can build a house. It actually shares the same process and structure with the traditional construction method. That's why villagers find it very handy. Once the structure is set up, the infill and its use can vary.

We simplified the means of communication as well. Our construction drawings for one building type are drawn on only 10 A4 pages. Usually in contemporary practice, the drawing set would cover at least 200 pages. The way of designing and communicating is close to the method of the traditional craftsmen. However, the lightweight steel structure can be industrialized and digitized.

I would like to provide three examples of its use. The first project is the reconstruction of Yangliu Village in Mao County in Sichuan Province after the earthquake. The mountain village had 56 households, and most of the residents are Qiang people, one of the ethnic minorities in China. Their original village houses use stone and wood from the mountains, a traditional construction method that they were able to maintain with the help of the lightweight steel structural frame. We provided the structure and let them finish the rest in their own way. Although the steel structural frames are similar, you won't find two houses that look alike, since the system as well as the material infill is flexible.

The second project is the reconstruction of a village in Taiwan after a flood in 2009. There, we rebuilt around 1,000 houses. Due to limited funds, the government didn't allow the villagers the freedom to make fundamental changes, or to build the infill themselves, as in the first case. However, we still built the houses but left the opportunity for the villagers to adjust or build some additional parts, such as terraces or gardens to promote ownership and diversity.

The third project happened recently in Xichuan, Henan Province. Because Beijing's water supply comes from this region, the environmental standards are higher than average. As mentioned previously, the government usually develops the rural areas in China by transplanting the concept of the urban or suburban community to the village. The village has a long history, rich culture, and a welldeveloped water system. We proposed increasing the density of the village while preserving the original village structure. We kept the vegetable gardens attached to the village houses and renovated most of the old buildings. Additionally, we designed a toilet separating urine and feces so that waste could be used as manure for the vegetable garden and farmland.

The examples demonstrate how the lightweight steel structure can be assembled in many different ways, using all kinds of materials, including those from traditional buildings. By doing so, it allows us to react to different conditions and processes. In addition, it won't cost more than a house built with simple materials in the easiest way. Prototypes can include shops, a teahouse, toilet, or a bridge. The 200-meter-long teahouse designed in Ya'an, next to the Ancient TeaRoute, is currently under construction. Because of its length and width, even with 500 customers at the same time, you still feel that there is only you and several of your friends!

Now let's consider aesthetics, which is more interesting for most architects. Many people will find diversity, and complexity in architecture beautiful, but do you know how tiring it is to achieve diversity since architects never want to let go of their design control? I would like to end with a story.

One of my friends came up with an idea for a pavilion for the 2009 Shenzhen Biennale exhibition. He asked two architects (including me) to join him. Together we made a sketch design. However, we just couldn't manage it ourselves, so we invited a young man from Sichuan, who also had a lot of ideas, which made it even more complicated... In the end we asked for advice from construction workers we just met. But they all had their own ideas too. This led to the team and the name for us, "The Weak."

Finally, we built something on a ruin close to the city center of Shenzhen. And then totally lost control over it—nobody knew what it was and nobody could even describe its shape. After two years even the grasses developed their own opinion and expression. So in the end we stated: "It is not easy to understand what and who *the others* are. But to understand this is the basic requirement for modern architects trying to work in rural areas today."

This article is an edited transcript from the Homecoming Symposium, April 13, 2012.

◄ Inner facade
of the Rural Tulou.

Typologies of Post-Ruralism

Interpretation of Chinese Urbanism
in the Urban Tulou and the Dafen Museum

by Urbanus Research Bureau

Transferring Typologies

The demarcation between urban and rural is a manmade concept. Urbanism refers to those manmade artifacts that generate density and accumulate resources, either socioeconomically or ecologically. The leftovers are recognized as rural and are always primitive and undeveloped. However, the Urban Tulou project and the urban village phenomenon deconstruct this oversimplified demarcation between the urban and the rural and offer strategies that blur the edge between these two concepts, remixing them to solve our urban and rural problems.

Urban villages evolved from bottom-up, informal strategies of survival, while the Urban Tulou project was formally directed as a top-down strategy to invoke informal methods of adaptive living. Urban villages, originally farming villages, grew hyper-densely and organically within a confined area, within the enveloping cityscape, evolving over several decades through many layers of occupancy and land-use policy transitions. The Urban Tulou was imported anachronistically: it was uprooted from its place of origin (literally as an utopian idea, meaning without place), and plunked down into a carefully planned alien land. The term *uprooted* certainly pertains to both typologies. For the urban village, the farmlands were conscripted for new city fabric, land-use rights were forced to conform to urban standards, indigenous landowners had to navigate treacherous land-grab negotiations, and tenants were forced out in mass evictions during inevitable redevelopment stages. For the Urban Tulou, although the typology was extracted from its original rural context, its aims are to re-root transitory populations into the context of urban hyperdensity.

Rural Typology in Urbanism

The *tulou*, or earth tower, developed by Hakka villagers, introduced an alternative, condensed typology for rural China, in order to accumulate foods and enhance defense. We recognize it as a process of typological transfer utilizing an urban typology to solve a rural problem. Urbanus designers were inspired by this concept of typological transfer, adapted the idea, and proposed the Urban Tulou project for low-income social classes in urban China. Interestingly, it is still an enclave for the rural population, or more precisely, for the floating population of migrant workers. The Urban Tulou is an experimental process to further push the idea of typological transfer. This was done by inverting an urban typology as a solution for a rural context into a post-rural typology as a solution to an urban context. The intention of the Urban Tulou is to remix urbanism and ruralism through blurring the boundary between them.

Rural Landscape in Urbanism

Instead of pluggingin rural landscapes into the city, the urban village is really a phenomenon about the displacement of processes typically attributed to the city fringe. The urban village can be recognized as a fringe condition even though it is sometimes located within the city center. In Shenzhen there are 320 urban villages ensconced within the city fabric, and although the typology of the urban village originates from a rural farming village, the untrained eye might not be able to recognize this fact because they have been assimilated into the city urban fabric. However, they still carry very different land-use rights and vestiges from different eras of policy making. Being the stepping-stone to adapt to more institutionalized city life, the informal density of social activities makes sense to the farmer migrants when they first arrive in the city. This stepping-stone for rural migrants is similar to the opportunities provided by the Urban Tulou project. Indeed, the Urban Tulou project was inspired by the urban village phenomenon.

The study of Dafen village is a key example that illustrates how intensive social networking facilitates business and the everyday life of migrants. In the early 1990s, a Hong Kong art dealer set up the first painting-related business in this village in order to take advantage of the relatively cheap rent and quiet village environment. Eventually, the success of this Hong Kong art dealer attracted many villagers from Shenzhen and other cities to learn painting. Currently, the village cluster has a population of 10,000 people in an area no bigger than 0.4 square kilometers. Almost of all of them are migrants. The counterfeiting painting industry in Dafen is self-organized by migrant painters from all over China. The knowledge transfer of counterfeit painting is based on a social network of referrals—many of the young painters are connected to the older painters as they originate from the same hometown. This social or family networking referral system is very similar to how migrant workers refer their relatives from rural areas to work in the same factory as them. Dafen is not only an urbanized village artifact, but more importantly it demonstrates the sustenance of the rural societal structure in urbanism.

Post-Rural Solutions to New Urbanism

Both of these projects react to the concept of post-ruralism—the transfer of a (post-)rural typology to urbanism. The Urban Tulou project and the Dafen Museum project share one objective: to blur the boundary between the formal and the informal in urban China. Indeed, the necessity of such a demarcation is questionable, even though Chinese society was historically structured by Mao into separate systems of governance for rural and urban. In the Urban Tulou project the architectural design provides a grayzone for the integration between rural migrants and the urbanity of modern life in China. On the other hand, the Dafen Museum project facilitates the informal activities associated with the rural within the urban village. Despite their differences both projects utilize *ruralism* as a design thinking methodology to solve urban problems. The approach is the antithesis to conventional urban problem solving strategies. The remix between these two concepts opens up a dualistic philosophical framework for our built environment.

▲ Rural Tulou.

▲ Rural landscape
in urbanism:
Dafen Urban
Village with Dafen
Art Museum.

▲ Rural typology
in urbanism:
Urban Tulou
replicated in
Shenzhen.

▲ Inner facade
of the Urban Tulou.

▶ Rural migrants
living in the Urban
Tulou.

D

◄ Rural migrants in Dafen Village, Shenzhen, painting idyllic rural scenes that are mass produced for hotels, lift lobbies, and offices around the world.

with Joshua Bolchover, Yung Ho Chan, Frank Dikötter, Juan Du, Huang ShengYuan, Hsieh Ying-chun, Hua Li, John Lin, Meng Yan, Cole Roskam, Tong Ming, Robin Visser, Wang Weijen, Zhang Ke, and Zhu Tao

Romanticizing the Rural
—Or—
The Countryside Never Speaks for Itself

John Lin: Are we in danger of romanticizing the rural?

Frank Dikötter: In 1949 in China, a registration system (*hukou*), separated citizen rights between the rural and the urban, creating a complete gap between the people in the city and the people in the countryside. Villagers were literally second-class citizens at best, and slaves at worst, right up until 1962. During the Great Leap Forward, orders were sent from the cities to tell farmers how they should grow their rice: "Close cropping, you should crop it very closely!" What strikes me is that again and again, based on the archives we are able to see, farmers were told what they should do by people in the city—how to plough land, or how to farm rice. And that has not changed. It is again people from the city, including architects, that seem to know what's best for the countryside. I think it's intrinsically related to not only this enormous gap between *Shi Min* (citizen) and *Nong Min* (farmer or peasant), but also to the political mechanisms of the one-party state.

Cole Roskam: Because the countryside is spoken for, it can maintain an ideal position, it can be romanticized. The countryside never speaks for itself. It's a recurring theme that has been constantly projected upon the countryside throughout the twentieth century. In the Republican Era pre-1949 this is by urban-based elites such as Liang Sicheng, who project their own imaginations upon the countryside. There is a risk to continue this process of projection: what an architect imagines the rural to be rather than what it is.

Robin Visser: In terms of the long-standing cultural emphasis on the rural in China, I think we can remember Fei Xiaotong's book *Xiang tu Zhongguo.* He wrote it in 1947 to a Shanghainese intellectual audience to remind them of their rural roots and of the nation's rural roots. But I think it's more than just nostalgia. Maybe I am speaking from personal experience. I lived in Xixiang Tang, a rural area outside of Nanning, which is the capital of Guangxi. I lived there from 1987 to 1989. I had to use ration tickets to collect food. We had to stand in line. There were a lot of electricity outages. To eat, you had to ride your bicycle to the market: slaughter chickens, skin fish. It was a very labor-intensive lifestyle, even for me as a foreign teacher at that time. However, what you did experience was a sense of coordinating your body's rhythms with the rhythms of nature, and the experience of a communal social structure that was embedded in a rural form of organization. And it took me, as an urban American, a while to adjust to that new way of living. But there was a sense of well-being that came from living in that way, despite thinking what I might have been missing intellectually. It is a mental construct in a sense, but when I focused on what I was experiencing, there was a real sense of contentment. When things started to change so rapidly in the 1990s and 2000s many of my friends felt that something got lost through this new form of urbanization. It wasn't just from a sense of nostalgia, something was culturally and socially lost in this transformation.

John Lin: Recently Wang Shu won the Pritzker Prize, which leads me to the question: What is the line between being identified as a Chinese architect and a contemporary architect? Should we be working towards the notion of a Chinese identity in architecture? Zhang Ke, you seem to have a little bit of angst over the labeling of *Chineseness*. Do you experience a pressure on Chinese architects that their work cannot just be contemporary, but that there has to be an aesthetic quality that defines it as being Chinese?

Zhang Ke: I do not agree with the understanding of *Chineseness*—I think it doesn't exist. China is a country with extreme diversity —it's ridiculous to talk about a ubiquitous form of Chineseness. And also an *explicit* Chineseness, or so-called *new* Chineseness, is a fallacy. It's projected by foreign observers who are anxious and eager to see something new and recognizably Chinese. If you really seek Chineseness, it is not something that comes from a formal language, but comes from a spirit of the Song Dynasty or the Ming Dynasty in terms of refinement or precision. There are a lot of things we can draw from, but those are not the things we see now. There is space to explore rather than try to define an immediate, fast-consuming, recognizable Chineseness as a form.

Aiming for Continuity and Coexistence
—*Or*—
There is No Material that is More Modern than Others

John Lin: Yung Ho commented that there is no such thing as contemporary materials or traditional materials. I disagree. Do you believe that materials do not have, or come with, an inherent political or even vernacular connotation? It seems that some of the architects use materiality to provide social critique or meaning in their projects. Tong Ming's project (No.Zhongshan Road, Hangshou) deals with the question of what not to destroy: it is more a problem of controlling destruction of the tile rather than construction. Yung Ho, your pavilion in Jinhua [Jinhua Park Pavilion 17, Jinhua] has a direct link to the vernacular, but the use of the irregular cladding subverts this link. Also, I think your adoration of plastics is based on the idea that plastics represent something very alien when coupled with something vernacular. Or Zhang Ke, in your Tibet projects you use local materials only. And Hsieh chooses one material for the structure —steel—and then the choice of infill material is purposefully left open to be defined by the villagers themselves. So I'm wondering can material choice and use be used in a political, social manner?

Tong Ming: I think everybody here believes that material itself is neutral. It must be connected to society, the era, and context.

The difference in our approaches as architects is how we do that. As an architect you know that you have a choice, the knowledge, the practice, the experience, and a lot of memories, a lot of sensibilities. So during the design process the architect does very different things. And one acts based on an aesthetic reason—in my view the only reason for architecture.

Yung Ho Chang: We know that certain materials are associated with specific periods of culture and so on. I think the danger is if one believes materials have meanings. You very likely end up seeing what we have seen all over: materials are used as wallpaper. I am talking from my own experience. Even if you use rammed earth—nobody knows how to build vernacularly anymore. The use of the material does not bring the ancient craft back. We have to use contemporary technology and our knowledge of other materials to remake it.

Zhang Ke: I agree with Yung Ho's comment about the non-discrimination of materials. There is no material that is more modern than others. There are always endless possibilities for us to rediscover the performance of materials, be it light or even smell. For me it is not about showing off the material, but rather using material as a way to trigger sensitivities and sometimes memories in a subtle way. This can create continuity. I think the keywords we should address in the discussion regarding material within the rural-urban transformation are *continuity* and *coexistence*. In terms of architecture, I totally believe that aiming for continuity and coexistence is possible.

The Countryside is also a Battlefield
—*Or*—
The Rural is a Form of Resistance

John Lin: Meng Yan described the rural as a battlefield, whilst for Huang ShengYuan the rural is almost a dream condition. It seems you [Huang ShengYuan] have made a clear choice towards a rural ideal, while Meng Yan needed to escape back to the city! I am interested in how the use and inspiration of the rural is potentially a form of resistance against conventional forms of practice? This also implies a more general question of how do you define resistance in your practice?

Huang ShengYuan: I think the countryside is also a battlefield. Everything we do will remain for a long time. So we fight and discuss a lot—especially between ourselves. In Taiwan, the countryside was ruined. Only recently is it on its way to being reconstructed. Nowadays, the younger generation has better ways of looking at their environment. They are confident and they want to enjoy their lives. My generation is a fighting generation. I found trust in the younger generation and I prefer learning from them, not as a form of resistance, but as encouragement for the future.

Meng Yan: We always have been trying hard to balance the needs of different parties. Developers are developers, they are not *Lei Feng* [selfless and modest], they are not going to help you for free—this is not in their nature. And the city has its own agenda. As architects we are caught in the middle. This is a very dangerous position. Of course you can help developers achieve what they want. Or you can stand on the government's side, or on the public's side, telling people: "No, I'm not going to do this." In some cases, like in the Caiwuwei project, on which we have been working for over a year, we were in the middle; we were in a very fragile situation. We don't want to be part of the developer team that would end up harming public values and we believe our primary role is to mediate.

Wang Weijen: I think we can resist through continuing a building tradition like Hua Li, or like Huang ShengYuan, who has dedicated his work and life to the countryside. Those are methods of resistance. Even trying to build a school differently is resistance, because in most cases you have to argue with the school officials who are primarily looking for ways in which they can manage the school, which is not based on quality of space. Simply dividing a big school into smaller school blocks causes huge discussions. We are all building spaces according to our education and values. So everything is a form of resistance when you are practicing as an architect.

Zhu Tao: I don't deny that architects can have visions, but architects indulge themselves in arenas of self-importance, such as biennale exhibitions and media publications. In the end one's voice becomes more or less irrelevant. Urbanization is so complex. It needs different disciplinary collaborations with social scientists, planners, and engineers. I believe both artistic imagination and also an empirical working methodology are needed. For example: many architects celebrate the notion of the *green* building. Whenever they introduce a building it is "sustainable or green," but there is rarely any empirical data or evaluation about the building's actual performance. It is up to the architect's personal, conceptual interpr-

etation. That's a problem! We don't have feedback for engaging research into the design process.

Zhang Ke: Of course we are no longer as naive and idealistic as the 1920s modernist movement to think that we can save the world. However, this is still not an excuse to shake off responsibility. I do not like to be in a battlefield without a vision. I do not like to talk about resistance only. We have to think more proactively, more positively to find answers for the challenges in front of us.

Cole Roskam: I don't think *resistance* is necessarily a very constructive term either. I think architects deny, they ignore, they enable, they facilitate, but I think this idea of resistance is too romantic and it still has a lingering association with the modernist ideal. If architects can imagine themselves as part of these mechanisms rather than trying to construct some kind of heroic work as a form of resistance, then one can define one's position through other terms, such as enabling and facilitating, which are much more optimistic positions for an architectural practice.

The Difference Between Us and Them
—*Or*—
Does the Countryside Really Need Architects?

Hua Li: After we finished the construction for the Museum of Handicraft the secretary of Tengchong City came to the village telling us that the government was planning to invest 20 million RMB to build a New Socialist Village. We were afraid that if this occurred and the village was designed by somebody who didn't care it would be a disaster. Architects always think they can do better, right? But I wonder: Does the countryside really need architects? Maybe the villagers can do it in their own way. This could be a chance to continue and evolve the given situation. The government only needs to invest the money. A new development doesn't have to be designed from the outside, it can be done by the villagers—from the inside. I think this is the question behind Hsieh Ying-chun's presentation and work: "What is the architect's role in rural practice?"

Meng Yan: I had a very interesting discussion with Li Xiaodong the other day—he gave a lecture in our office. It was all about the position of the architect. He showed us many beautiful buildings that made me jealous. The sites and projects he chose to show us were so beautiful, so nice, so picturesque. Unfortunately, we [Urbanus] have never had the chance to work on such beautiful sites. All our sites have been extremely ugly so far. Later on, he also showed us a couple of urban projects (ugly sites with less perfect buildings), and he said that he just doesn't want to be part of *that* and what he really wants is to find the perfect place in remote Yunnan under the snow mountains. It seems so easy to make beautiful architecture there because of this amazing landscape. It is such a set, a theater. To me, that is problematic. If some architects work on those sites, it's of course fine, but it shouldn't be a trend for Chinese architects. We have so many problems in front of us! We cannot escape and retreat just to create beautiful architecture without facing reality and its challenges. This is what we [Urbanus] have been fighting for many years. I think this is why I wouldn't care about whether it's rural or urban—it doesn't really matter. But where there is a problem, an issue, I will go for it, I will face it! I think

this is an active role. Hua Li talked about using the government's money to distribute it to villagers, to build for themselves, instead of constructing a Socialist New Village. I'm worried about that too: if you have seen the examples in Hangzhou, in Zhejiang, where local villagers have built all these Disneyland houses. There is no basic understanding of tradition and locality anymore, because history has been discontinued. Tradition is not tenable for a lot of these villagers anymore.

Tong Ming: Throughout the presentation today, we saw many aspects of the rural: the beautiful countryside, but also the incredibly fast development and transformation of this landscape. Instead of distinguishing the urban and the rural as two different entities, I would rather distinguish these terms as different states of production: summarizing the status of production of the urban as industrialized production, and the status of the rural as pre-industrialized production. What does this mean? The industrialized status is driven by machine production, but the pre-industrialized status is driven by human [handmade] production. I think these two kinds of status exist both within the city and the countryside. This means, even within the city, we cannot escape from pre-industrialized production. Where can architects position themselves within this model? If architects only exist in the pre-industrialized status, there would be no difference between the architect and the farmer. We saw the bamboo house masterpiece, in the presentation of Hua Li, accomplished by an anonymous farmer! What is the difference between us and them? Maybe the architect is the person who does the job consciously. I am not pessimistic, because both modes will always exist next to each other. The pressure of the current situation is that the status of one area is developing too quickly.

These Days the Rural Is Entirely Consumed by the Urban
—Or—
Most of Our Cities Are Built by Farmers

Joshua Bolchover: Frank Dikötter left us with a very strong image of the Chinese countryside as a site of neglect and of horrific violence that took place during the Mao period. How do you see the Chinese country-side today? How has it changed since 1978, and what are your views on its future?

Hua Li: This is a Wen Jiabao question. I can only speak from my personal experience working on the Museum of Handicraft Paper in Yunnan. What I learned and realized from that project is that the countryside is under constant transformation. Young people intend to escape the countryside because agriculture is simply not profitable. This is the case for almost every village in China. To attract young villagers to stay you need something that can evolve from daily life: for example, the profession of paper-making. If nobody improves or innovates this skill, the traditional craft will die out. Tradition is also a process under constant transformation —it is not static. And this extends not only to paper-making, but also to other fields, such as building technology. For example: younger people are not willing to learn how to build timber constructions, as it is not very profitable and also very labor-intensive. So they run away to find a better solution. It's a very complicated issue and an endemic problem of the countryside.

Meng Yan: When I was a kid, at the end of the Cultural Revolution, we were asked to go to the countryside to learn to work in the fields. It was basic training involving manual work. Looking at it in a positive way, it was like an engaging workshop. Of course at that time we were forced to go; however, it was a good experience to get familiar with the countryside, its people, and to learn new skills. Compared with this early experience of the countryside, the meaning of the rural has changed completely. Nowadays, the rural condition is very hard to understand and to digest. Last year, I was in Henan Province, on a trip from one of the very old Song Dynasty cities where the Song imperial tomb was found, to some other places. But for some reason we got lost as we left the highway and went directly into the countryside. And what we found was shocking. We were in the middle of nowhere, with more than a hundred small chimneystacks billowing yellowish and grayish smoke. You could not see much through the car window, it was so dusty. We felt like we were in a movie! The only thing we could think of was: "How can we escape this place as quickly as possible?" Advertisements along the road from Gongyi to Songshan told us what they were producing. The entire village produces what we use every day in architecture: a fire-proofing material. You find around 50 small factories in a single village. That's what is happening in the rural areas and I was shocked. I thought I had found myself back in 1958 witnessing the Great Leap Forward right in front of me. In this situation, I realized that these days the rural is entirely consumed by the urban.

Zhang Ke: I'm less interested in the comparison between the current condition and the past. I'm more interested in imagining what will happen in the future—in the next five to ten years. The new central government plan will invest 4,000 billion RMB in agriculture and infrastructure in the next five years alone. This will have a big impact on the environment—350 million farmers will either move into the city or will be urbanized on-site. There will be a huge transformation in the next five years. Meng Yan, if you think your practice is only urban—pretty soon you probably will be involved in the rural!

Zhu Tao: I suggest to everyone to read the 12th Five-Year Plan of the central government. This blueprint is underway right now. By the end of the year 2030 China will reach 70% urbanization rate. Last year [2011] it was 50%. That means we need to increase the urbanization rate by 1% every year. And to make that process even more concrete, by the year 2025 China needs to move 350 million people from a rural population to an urban one, either to existing cities or to newly built ones. What's the scale? The whole United States population has a population of only 310 million. That means China moves an entire country with a larger population than the United States in less than 20 years! With the current, conventional practice model of the architect, based on either the individual liberal artist or the collective studio, I would say architects can design good objects, but we can't confuse designing good objects with the issue of urbanization in China. Therefore, given the architectural practice model is limited, we need to open up or unfold other platforms for this urgently needed research and discussion. Planners are hectic, officials are also hectic, and the ability of architects, who are probably critical, is inadequate. I think essentially the University has to play that role and become more involved.

Hsieh Ying-chun: The Chinese countryside is on a scale that is unprecedented—it is like another world. From Huang ShengYuan's practice you can tell that he is very optimistic.

But I'm not. What we try to do is rescue a tiny part of the countryside. Currently, we are asked to finish the plan for one village in only one day, which of course is completely absurd. In the next Five-Year Plan most of the rural villages will be reconstructed. This is scary to think about—350 million rural inhabitants will be moved to new houses. This is a very pessimistic scenario. Well, I am going to tell you a scenario that is more optimistic. You may not know about the two-pipe sewage system. It is a sewage system that separates solid and liquid waste. I recommended the two-pipe sewage system to one village. Without water the excrement quickly accumulates and becomes fertilizer. The method is developed by the United Nations and is very clean. The village government official accepted the idea, but the current land division in the village did not allow the use of this system. There was simply not enough land. The only way was to intersperse the vegetable plots with the housing sites. By doing this, the housing density was reduced and the fecal pollution problem solved. Furthermore, it offers a typical rural life style. Apart from the centralized arable land, the vegetable plots are attached to the housing and form a basic, rural, self-sustained unit. After a short discussion the village government official agreed to this model (I told him the Communist Party's People's Liberation Army is good at penetration and thrust tactics—that's how they beat the Nationalist Army). He understood the metaphor, attached the vegetable plots to the housing sites and introduced the two-pipe sewage system. That's what Ebeneezer Howard meant with "Garden Cities": the combination of agricultural production and dwelling. I believe that optimistic and pessimistic conditions coexist together in this process.

Juan Du: UNESCO has reported this year that the urban population finally exceeded the rural population. China will reach 70% urban population in the next 30 years. And this is not only the case in China—it's very much a global trend. I think rather than the nostalgic term of "let's resist urbanization," or buying into "urbanization equals destruction," we can find new strategies. This dichotomy, the oppositions we keep setting up, such as "Cities are dense and polluted" and the "Countryside is beautiful and picturesque," no longer exist. It is always fiction: all rural lands are engineered landscapes; agriculture itself is actually extremely polluting and uses the greatest amount of water in the world. Our cities right now are more and more populated by rural residents who were formerly farmers and most of our cities are built by farmers. There is really no one who was born in the city who is building the city. So from a social perspective the rural and urban really do blur.

Joshua Bolchover: That is a good way to end. I think it is clear that the agenda we are trying to set out is that the future of rural-urban territory is clearly an urgent and critical issue in China. It is one that needs more investigation, either through academia or through the architect becoming more actively involved in the definition of this new territory through innovative modes of practice.

▲ Urbanizing the rural: scarred landscapes and new development zones.

Appendix

People

Joshua Bolchover is an Assistant Professor at The University of Hong Kong and Director of Rural Urban Framework (RUF). His current research focuses on emergent urban transformation. He has exhibited at the Chengdu Biennale 2011 and at the Venice Biennale 2010. The building projects have been published in *Vitamin Green* (Phaidon, 2012), *Moderators of Change* (Hatje Cantz, 2011), and the *Architectural Review*, winning a high commendation in the AR+D Emerging Architecture Awards 2012. His urban strategy for Hong Kong's border zone has been exhibited at the Hong Kong-Shenzhen Biennale 2011 and at the Venice Biennale 2008. He has curated, designed, and contributed to several other international exhibitions, including *Get it Louder*, 2007; *Airspace: What Skyline Does London Want?* 2006; and *Can Buildings Curate*, 2005. Between 2003 and 2005 he was a local curator for the Manchester-Liverpool section of the Shrinking Cities international research project. He has previously taught architecture at the Chinese University of Hong Kong, London Metropolitan University, Cambridge University, and the Architectural Association. He was educated at Cambridge University and at the Bartlett School of Architecture. *www.rufwork.org*

Yung Ho Chang is a Chinese-American architect and the Head Professor of MIT Architecture. He studied at the Nanjing Institute of Technology (now Southeast University) before he went to the United States where he received his MArch from the University of California, Berkeley, and went on to teach in the U.S. for the next 15 years before returning to Beijing to establish China's first private architecture firm, Atelier FCJZ. He has exhibited internationally as an artist as well as architect and is widely published, including the monograph *Yung Ho Chang/Atelier Feichang Jianzhu: A Chinese Practice*. His interdisciplinary research focuses on the city, materiality, and tradition. He often combines his research activities with design commissions. Before taking up his position at MIT, he also served as the Kenzo Tange Chair Professor at the Harvard Graduate School of Design as well as the Eliel Saarinen Chair Professor at the University of Michigan. *www.fcjz.com*

Frank Dikötter is the author of *Mao's Great Famine: The History of China's Most Devastating Catastrophe*, published by Bloomsbury and Walker Books. The book was selected as one of the Books of the Year in 2010 by *The Economist*, *The Independent*, the *Sunday Times*, the *London Evening Standard*, *The Telegraph* and the *New Statesman*. It also won the 2011 Samuel Johnson Prize for Non-Fiction, Britain's most prestigious book award for non-fiction. Frank Dikötter has been Chair Professor of Humanities at the University of Hong Kong since 2006. Before coming to Hong Kong he was Professor of the Modern History of China at the School of Oriental and African Studies, University of London. He has published nine books that have changed the ways historians view modern China, from the classic *The Discourse of Race in Modern China* (1992) to *China before Mao: The Age of Openness* (2007). *www.Dikotter.com*

Juan Du is Associate Professor and Director of the MArch Program in the Department of Architecture at the University of Hong Kong and the founding director of IDU_architecture. Her work has been exhibited internationally, including at the Venice Biennale International Architecture Exhibition, Vienna Architekturzentrum Exhibition, the Brazil International Exhibition of Architecture, and the Beijing Biennale. She was the Chief Curator of Hong Kong's participation in the 2010 Venice Biennale of Architecture, Curator of the *Housing an Affordable City* exhibition at the 2011 Shenzhen & Hong Kong Bi-City Biennale, and the Assistant Curator for the First Shenzhen Biennale of Urbanism/Architecture in 2005. She has published internationally, including in *China Voices*, *Urban Trans_Formations*, *Domus International*, *Urban China*, and the *Journal of Architectural Education*. She has taught Architectural and Urban Design at the Department of Architecture of MIT and the Graduate Center of Architecture at Peking University. She holds a master's degree in architecture from Princeton University and is the recipient of a Fulbright Scholarship for her research on the transformations of the contemporary Chinese city. *www.iduarchitecture.com*

Cruz Garcia is a Puerto Rican architect, artist, and writer who graduated from the Universidad de Puerto Rico. In 2008 he cofounded WAI Architecture Think Tank with Nathalie Frankowski. He is an Associate Partner at Standardarchitecture.

Huang ShengYuan visited the Taiwanese countryside 17 years ago. Falling in love with the scenery and culture he stayed and opened his own practice Fieldoffice. Since then, he has dedicated himself to rural landscape architecture. He and his team have been recipients of awards, including the Green Architectural Design Award and the Taiwan Architecture Award. *www.fieldoffice.com.tw*

Hsieh Ying-chun is a Taiwanese architect and contractor. He graduated from Tam-king Architecture Department in 1977. He founded Hsieh Architects and Associates in 1984 and designed numerous high-technology factories and public buildings, followed by the Xin-zhu County Cultural Center in 1997 and Mei-nong Hakka Museum in 1998. Since 1999 Hsieh Ying-chun has played a key role in rebuilding communities for indigenous communities after Taiwan's devastating earthquake in 1999. Since then he has cofounded Atelier-3 and Rural Architecture Studio. Having worked as a contractor in the first stage of his professional life, for him, the reconstruction of housing and communities are charged with two challenges: to build houses within an extremely tight budget and to base the projects on the notion of sustainable construction, green building, cultural preservation and the creation of local employment opportunities. Hsieh represented Taiwan in the Venice Architecture Biennale 2006 and Venice Biennale of Contemporary Art 2009 and was awarded with the Curry Stone Design Prize in 2011. *www.atelier-3.com*

Christiane Lange is a Visiting Assistant Professor in the Department of Architecture, at the University of Hong Kong. Her research and interest addresses the urbanization process of developing countries. Her design emphasis is placed on strategies that support and define sustainability from the city to the village. She contributed her urban research and design work about Addis Ababa, Ethiopia, and Schwyz, Switzerland, to the

Venice Biennale in 2008. Since 2008 she has collaborated with Jörg Stollmann and Rainer Hehl on Urbaninform. Urbaninform has built an online platform featuring sustainable urban development projects that negotiate top-down planning and civil society commitment. Urbaninform organizes competitions, network events, podium discussions and contributed to the IABR Rotterdam 2009, the WUF Rio de Janeiro 2010, and to the Small Scale, Big Change exhibition at the Museum of Modern Art (MOMA) in New York 2010. She was educated at the HTWK Leipzig and the ETH Zürich.

Hua Li is the founder and principal of TAO (Trace Architecture Office). He received his MArch from Yale University in 1999 and his BArch from Tsinghua University in 1994. He has worked at Westfourth Architecture and Herbert Beckhard Frank Richlan & Associates in New York. In 2003 he returned to China and started his own practice in Beijing. Since 2004, Hua Li has taught at the Central Academy of Fine Arts and has been a visiting critic at the School of Architecture in Tsinghua University. In 2009, he established TAO. Hua Li's design works have been published by numerous architectural media, including *T+A*, *WA*, *Domus*, *Area*, *A+U*, *MD*, *Wallpaper**, *Abitare*, *Arquitectura Viva (AV)*, *Casabella*, and *Space*. *www.t-a-o.cn*

John Lin is currently Director of Rural Urban Framework (RUF) and an Assistant Professor at the University of Hong Kong. After studying in both the art and engineering programs at The Cooper Union in New York City, he received a professional degree in architecture in 2002. His research concerns the process of urbanization in rural areas with a focus on the sustainable development of Chinese villages. With RUF his projects have been exhibited internationally, including at the Venice Biennale of Architecture and the MAK Vienna. His House For All Seasons was the winner of the 2012 Architecture Review House Award, the 2012 WA Chinese Architecture Award, and a finalist in the 2012 China Architecture Media Award under the category Best Habitation. He has received three AR Awards for Emerging Architecture, in 2009, 2010, and 2012. His work has been published in *Architectural Record*, *Architectural Review*, *Mark*, *Domus*, *Frame*, and *A+U*. He has taught previously at the Royal Danish Academy of Fine Arts, School of Architecture and the Chinese University of Hong Kong. He is the 2010 recipient of the Outstanding Teaching Award at the University of Hong Kong. *www.rufwork.org*

Liu Jiakun graduated from Chongqing University School of Architecture. After graduating, Liu Jiakun worked at the Chengdu Design and Research Institute in Tibet and Xinjiang. He established his own design studio, Jiakun Architects, in 1999, and started working on projects mainly in China, devoting himself to the earthquake reconstruction in Sichuan Province. Jiakun Architects took part in the Venice Architecture Biennale 2008, the Chinese Young Architects' Work Exhibition in Germany, the Chinese Contemporary Architecture Exhibition in France, NAI China Contemporary Architecture and many other international exhibitions. Liu Jiakun won the Honor Prize of the 7th ARCASIA, Chinese Architecture & Art Prize 2003, Architectural Record Magazine China Awards, Far East Award in Architecture and Architectural Design Award from Architectural Society of China. The projects of Jiakun Architects have been published by architectural magazines such as *A+U*, *AV*, *Area*, *Domus*, *MADE IN CHINA*, *AR*, *GA*, and others. *www.jiakun-architects.com*

Meng Yan cofounded Urbanus with his partners Liu Xiaodu and Wang Hui in 1999. Urbanus has become one of the most influential architectural design firms in China. Meng Yan is an architect licensed in New York State. He received his bachelor and master's degrees in architecture from Tsinghua University, and master's degree of architecture from Miami University. The design projects of Urbanus range from cultural, residential architecture to new urban public space, renovation of old urban areas, and civic and large-scale urban complexes. The works of Urbanus have been awarded numerous prestigious architecture prizes and have been exhibited and published worldwide. The partners are regularly invited to lecture at renowned universities and academies and to be jurors for international competitions. The Urbanus Research Bureau, which is primarily concerned with urban research, focuses on contemporary urban China to conduct a series of research projects, including creative city development, post-urban village development, and typologies for hyperdensity. *www.urbanus.com.cn*

Cole Roskam is an Assistant Professor of Architectural History and Theory in the Department of Architecture at the University of Hong Kong, where he teaches undergraduate, graduate, and post-graduate courses on topics in architectural and urban history. His research focuses on early-twentieth-century Chinese architectural history, colonial and postcolonial built environments in Asia, and architectural development in China since the Cultural Revolution. His writing has appeared in *Artforum* and *Orientations*. He is currently working on a book manuscript based upon his dissertation, *Civic Architecture in a Liminal City: Shanghai, 1842–1937*.

Philip Tinari is Director of the Ullens Center for Contemporary Art, an independent museum in Beijing's 798 Art District. Prior to joining UCCA in 2011, he was founding editor-in-chief of LEAP, a bilingual (Chinese-English) magazine of contemporary art published by the Modern Media Group. Tinari is a contributing editor to *Artforum* and worked previously as the China advisor to Art Basel. A resident of Beijing for much of the past decade, he has written and lectured widely on contemporary Chinese art. He holds an MA in East Asian studies from Harvard, a BA from the Literature Program at Duke, and was a Fulbright Scholar at Peking University. *www.ucca.org.cn*

Tong Ming is an Associate Professor in the Department of Urban Planning at Tongji University. He received his bachelor's and master's degrees in architecture from Southeast University in Nanjing, and a doctoral degree in urban planning from the College of Architecture and Urban Planning at Tongji University. Tong Ming focuses both on theoretical research and practical work in architecture and urban planning. He has published over 30 academic papers and books. He founded his architecture practice, TM Studio, in Shanghai in 1999.

Robin Visser is an Associate Professor of Asian Studies at the University of North Carolina at Chapel Hill, where she also serves as Interim Director of the Carolina Asia Center, Adjunct Associate Professor in the Department of English and Comparative Literature, and Faculty Fellow in the Center for Urban and Regional Studies. She received a BS in Mechanical Engineering from the University of Michigan before switching to Chinese Literature, in which she received an

MA at the University of Colorado and a PhD from Columbia University. She's received numerous fellowships and awards, including a Fulbright. Her recent book, *Cities Surround the Countryside: Urban Aesthetics in Postsocialist China*, was a Book Award Finalist at the Southeast Conference of the Association of Asian Studies in 2011.

Wang Weijen is a Professor at the Department of Architecture, at the University of Hong Kong. Weijen graduated from UC Berkeley and Taiwan University. His design projects won several AIA Design awards and the Far Eastern Architectural Award and have been exhibited at the Taipei Museum of Modern Art, Beijing Architecture Biennale, Shenzhen Biennale of Architecture and Urbanism, and the Venice Architecture Biennale of 2008. He was the curator of the Hong Kong–Shenzhen Biennale of Architecture and Urbanism 2007/2008. His research mainly focuses on Chinese architecture and cities. He was a Visiting Associate Professor at the Department of Architecture at MIT in 2008–09.
www.wwjarchitecture.com

Zhang Ke set up his practice, Standardarchitecture, in Beijing in 2001. He studied at Tsinghua University (1993) and at Harvard Graduate School (1996). Today, Standardarchitecture has, in a brief period of time, established a reputation as the Chinese avant-garde. In 2006, the architects were recognized with the first prize of the China Architecture Award. In 2009, they won the Best Young Architect Award of the first China Architecture Media Award (CAMA). The Yaluntzangpu Boat Terminal near Linzhi, Tibet, is among Standardarchitecture's most important projects.
www.standardarchitecture.cn

Zhu Tao is an Assistant Professor in Department of Architecture at the University of Hong Kong and a PhD candidate in Architecture History and Theory at Columbia University. He practices in China and writes on contemporary Chinese architecture and urbanism. His most recent writing works include a chapter "Architecture in China in the Reform Era 1978–2010" for the book *A Critical History of Contemporary Architecture 1960–2010* to be published in 2013.

Imagery

Works by Atelier-3, Fieldoffice, Jiakun Architects, Rural Urban Framework, Standardarchitecture, Trace Architecture Office, Urbanus, and Wang Weijen Architecture

Namchabawa Visitor Center
Linzhi, Tibet 2007–08
Standardarchitecture, Zhang Ke

Museum of Handicraft Paper
Yunnan, China 2011–12
Trace Architecture Office, Hua Li

House for all Seasons
Shaanxi, China 2010–12
Rural Urban Framework, John Lin

Hotel of Nanjing
CIPEA Nanjing, China 2005–ongoing
Jiakun Architects, Liu Jiakun

House for all Seasons
Shaanxi, China 2010–12
Rural Urban Framework, John Lin

Pedestrian Bridge
Yilan Revitalization, Yilan Taiwan 2008–ongoing
Fieldoffice, Huang ShengYuan

Village Mountains
Future Scenario China, 2007–ongoing
Standardarchitecture, Zhang Ke

Urban Tulou
Shenzhen, China 2005–08
Urbanus, Meng Yan

XiXi Waterland Art Village
Hangzhou, China, 2011–ongoing
Wang Weijen Architecture, Wang Weijen

Urban Tulou
Shenzhen, China 2005–08
Urbanus, Meng Yan

Rebirth Brick Proposal
Sichuan Earthquake 2008
China 2008–ongoing
Jiakun Architects, Liu Jiakun

**Yarluntzangbu Grand Canyon
Art Center**
Linzhi, Tibet 2010–11
Standardarchitecture, Zhang Ke

Dafen Art Museum & Dafen Village
Shenzhen, China 2005–07
Urbanus, Meng Yan

Niyang River Visitor Center
Linzhi, Tibet, 2009–11
Standardarchitecture, Zhang Ke